M

6/14

Tips a
When Selling
a Home

Other McGraw-Hill Books by Robert Irwin

Tips and Traps When Selling a Home

Robert Irwin

Third Edition

McGraw-Hill

New York   Chicago   San Francisco   Lisbon   London
Madrid   Mexico City   Milan   New Delhi   San Juan
Seoul   Singapore   Sydney   Toronto

Copyright © 2004 by The McGraw-Hill Companies, Inc. All rights reserved. Printed in the United States of America. Except as permitted under the United States Copyright Act of 1976, no part of this publication may be reproduced or distributed in any form or by any means, or stored in a data base or retrieval system, without the prior written permission of the publisher.

1 2 3 4 5 6 7 8 9 0   AGM/AGM   0 9 8 7 6 5 4 3

ISBN 0-07-141830-X

McGraw-Hill books are available at special quantity discounts to use as premiums and sales promotions, or for use in corporate training programs. For more information, please write to the Director of Special Sales, Professional Publishing, McGraw-Hill, Two Penn Plaza, New York, NY 10121-2298. Or contact your local bookstore.

This book contains the author's opinions. Some material in this book may be affected by changes in the law (or changes in interpretations of the law) or changes in the market conditions since the manuscript was prepared. Therefore, the accuracy and completeness of the information contained in this book and the opinions based on it cannot be guaranteed. Neither the author nor the publisher is engaged in rendering investment, legal, tax, accounting, or other similar professional services. If these services are required, the reader should obtain them from a competent professional. The publisher and the author hereby specifically disclaim any liability for loss incurred as a consequence of following any advice or applying information presented in this book

 This book is printed on recycled, acid-free paper containing a minimum of 50% recycled, de-inked fiber.

Library of Congress Cataloging-in-Publication Data

Irwin, Robert, 1941-
    Tips and traps when selling a home / by Robert Irwin.— 3rd ed.
      p. cm.
    Includes index.
    ISBN 0-07-141830-X (alk. paper)
    1. House selling. 2. Real estate business. I. Title.
HD1379.I674 2004
333.33'83—dc21
                          2003011669

CONTENTS

ACKNOWLEDGMENTS

Thanks to the many real estate professionals who provided input for this book, a special thanks to Jason Benjamin for his work in compiling data and fact checking, and, of course, love to and grateful appreciation for my wife, Reet, for putting up with me during all those early morning and late-night hours spent writing the text.

1
Sell Fast in Any Market

You want to sell your house. (Why else would you be checking out this book?)

You want to sell it fast. (Few people want their homes to languish on the market.)

You want to get as much money as you can from the sale. (Okay, who wants to sell their home for less than it's worth?!)

So, how do you do it?

How to Sell Your Home

There are five simple elements to selling any home in any market. Pay attention to all five, and you'll quickly have a sale for a good price.

Five Elements to Selling Your Home

1. Price
2. Location
3. Exposure
4. Appearance
5. Time

TIP—IT'S "PLEAT"!

If you're one of those who like acronyms to help jar your memory, you can easily refer to these five elements as PLEAT.

Price It Right, and Buyers Will Come

The rule in real estate is that you can sell any property for any price *if you wait long enough.*

It's largely a function of time and inflation. A seller is asking $200,000 for his property, even though agents tell him it's not worth more than $190,000. He tells the agents to take a flying leap and keeps his property for sale and on the market.

A year later, a buyer walks in and offers him his $200,000. "I told you so!" he says. But, has he really shown everyone that he was right? Or is it simply that after a year of inflation and price appreciation, the value of his property has finally moved up to what he was asking? If he had been willing to accept the true market value of the home at the time he put it up for sale, $190,000, he might have sold it immediately.

But, you may be saying, he waited and got $10,000 more!

Yes, but he could have bought another property in the same market and made a similar or greater profit. And in the meantime, he would have been long gone from the old house that he wanted to get rid of.

TIP—GET THE HIGH END OF THE PRICE RANGE

Even though the price is determined by the market, there's always a range of prices for any given house. Be sure that you're getting the top of the price range for your home. (Check into Chapter 3, where we go into that in great detail.)

Location, Location, Location!

Everyone knows that these are the three most important words in real estate. However, as a seller, you may think that they only apply to buyers and not realize that they apply to you as well.

You may think that your neighborhood is okay, only to realize that others don't feel the same way. For example, your neighborhood may have deteriorated during the time you've lived there and you haven't really noticed. Or a big, noisy lumber mill a half mile away may never have bothered you, but it turns off potential buyers.

You'll find out if the neighborhood is the problem because people will tell you. Agents will tell you. Home hunters who stop by will tell you (if you ask). Even some of your neighbors will tell you.

If it turns out that your house isn't selling because it's in a bad location, what can you do about it? The best thing you could have done was to have bought in a better neighborhood. (Remember this for next time!) However, since you have already bought, the one thing you cannot do is change your home's location. If there's a landfill nearby or a swampy river or a blighted area, you can't move your house somewhere else. You can, however, endeavor within certain limits to change the neighborhood.

For example, people who wanted to sell their homes but were unable to because of the Love Canal eventually got restitution. In southern California, in several instances homeowners have gotten landfill dumps closed. In other cases, sellers have created local homeowners' associations that have made efforts to clean up neighborhoods.

All these things take time and effort. However, if you're willing to do them, they can ultimately produce results for you in the form of a sale at a higher price.

You can also do other things, such as offering buyers better terms to compensate for the neighborhood. A good comparison here is automobiles in a used-car lot. You walk in, and, of course, you look at all the shiny models. But your wallet is a bit slim that day, and so you ask the dealer if there might not be a less expensive car available.

The dealer leads you to the back of the lot, where there's a car that looks okay, but the dealer says it has a broken air conditioner. He tells you that it will cost $1000 to fix it, and he'll take that amount off the price if you'll buy it as is.

Would you buy it?

Many people will, particularly if it's winter or if they live in a cooler climate where they can get by without air conditioning. Similarly, many people will buy in a worse neighborhood if they can get a better deal. In some cases they need the better deal in order to buy at all. In other cases they just like to get good deals.

When the neighborhood is bad, offer better terms.

Exposure—Are You Getting the Word Out?

Lack of exposure simply means that not enough buyers have been made aware of the fact that your home is for sale. There are several ways of tracking exposure.

How to Track Exposure

1. *Count the number of buyers who come through your house.* Counting heads is the easiest approach. Or you can have a little sign-in book at the door. If you haven't had a visit from a buyer in a week or more, it's a bad sign. On the other hand, if buyers keep coming through and looking, but there are no offers, you may have a different problem (see the other elements of selling).

2. *Count the number of real estate people who come through.* If you have your house listed, you should have caravans of agents coming through, particularly when the house first goes on the market. Whole offices of agents, when they become aware that your property has been listed, will come by to see it, to remember it, and to determine whether they any buyers for it. Later, individual agents will come by to see if your house is right for a particular buyer they have.

3. *Count the number of agents' cards.* When agents come by, they usually leave their business card. Count the cards. If there are only a few, it could mean trouble. Agents know that they can't see all the houses that are for sale; thus, they pick out the ones that they believe are most likely to be sellers. Few business cards means that they may be avoiding your house. Call your agent and ask if she or he has been "talking up" your house at agents' meetings. Ask if there is something you can do, such as offering a bonus to the selling agent, that will spark interest.

4. *Count the number of calls that you get.* If you're selling your house yourself, you undoubtedly have a sign out and an ad in the paper. If you do, you're bound to get calls. If those calls don't come in or there are very few of them, or if the potential buyers who call are confused about what you're selling or hang up when you explain what you've got, you may have a problem. Recheck your advertising for clarity and impact. Make sure that *you* call back everyone who rings you up.

5. *Check to see that your home is publicized.* Again, check with your agent to see that he or she is "talking up" your home to other agents. Watch for advertising of homes by your agent. Be sure that there are flyers in a box on your sign. Ask your agent what other venues he or she is pursuing in publicizing your home, including online exposure.

TRAP—DON'T LOOK FOR YOUR HOME TO BE ADVERTISED

Smart agents advertise price ranges, not individual homes. If your agent has ads running for homes in your price range, that's good enough. Chances are that buyers who call will be interested in your home. Don't insist that your house be the one that's advertised, since few buyers ever purchase the home that they initially call the agent about.

Appearance—Is Your House Shipshape for Selling?

Don't rely on your own opinion of your home's condition. (You're probably biased in favor of its current looks.) Get an expert to tell you. Call in an agent(s) and ask how the condition of your house compares with that of similar homes on the market.

Listen carefully to what is said, since most people, including agents, are hesitant to give offense. Listen for the dropped hints. For example, "Your house is lovely, except for that swamp of a pool in the backyard." Or, "No problems, except the carpeting has all those spots." Or, "It looks great and will look even better once you get a new roof on." Or, "Nothing wrong with it that a new coat of paint won't fix."

Take these comments to heart. Others often see the true condition of your property far more clearly than you, the owner, do. As sellers, we tend to overlook the bad and exaggerate the good. Potential buyers are not nearly so generous.

TIP—WORK ON THE "CURB APPEAL" OF YOUR HOME

Real estate agents recognize it as a fact of life that for buyers, first impressions count most. If your house looks beautiful when potential buyers drive up and first see it, those buyers are going to be favorably inclined toward the house, even if it's not perfect on the inside. This is called *curb appeal.* Make it work for you, not against you.

One of the things you can do is to drive by your home with friends or neighbors in the car and ask them what they initially see about your house that they like and don't like. Agents can also provide good clues here. Then take corrective measures. Often minor cosmetic changes, such as paint, a new lawn and shrubs, or a redone driveway, can make a world of difference.

Discover the problem and correct it, and you should be well on the way toward selling that house.

Time—Have You Given It Enough?

Remember that the average amount of time that it takes to sell a home differs with each market. You've put your home on the market, and it's been 4 weeks. Lots of would-be buyers have come by, but you've had no offers. What's the problem?

Maybe you just haven't given it enough time. Go to your agent and ask what is the average time it takes to sell a home in the current market. In the superheated market of the last few years, only a week or two in some areas may have been needed. Typically however, it's 2 to 6 months in most markets.

If the average time in your area is 2 months, then stop worrying. Just be patient. Chances are there simply hasn't been enough time for the right buyer to find your home.

TIP—FRESHNESS HELPS

The newer the listing, the easier it is to sell the house at full price. The longer you have your home on the market—the longer it "ages"—the more likely you are to get lowball offers. If your house hasn't sold after an appropriate amount of time, you might be wise to take it off the market for a few months and then put it back on later as a new, "fresh" listing.

TRAP—IT'S JUST AN AVERAGE

Remember that the average length of time for sale is just that, an average. Just as many houses take longer to sell as sell more quickly.

What about Market Conditions?

I'm sure some readers are wondering why I haven't included market conditions in the five elements. After all, in the recent superheated markets, a home might expect to sell in a few weeks. In the cold markets of the 1990s, it might have taken a year.

Actually, we have taken market conditions into account in several of the elements, such as price and time. However, it won't hurt for you to take a few moments to analyze your local real estate market.

If the market is still superheated, then you may want to up your price a bit beyond what recent sales indicate that your home is worth in order to catch the wave. On the other hand, if the market is terrible, you may want to lower your price in order to catch the wave going in the other direction.

What about Terms?

Finally, there's the matter of terms. This used to be a big issue when financing was difficult. Sellers who offered to carry back paper (a second mortgage) often found that they could get a quicker sale and more money.

Today, however, with excellent financing available for almost all buyers, terms aren't nearly as important. Most buyers expect to get a mortgage, put very little down, and pay cash to the seller.

However, in the future, if interest rates once again become high, terms could be a deciding element. When interest rates rise above about 8 percent, buyers find it much more difficult to purchase. In that kind of market, if you can offer lower-interest-rate financing by carrying back a mortgage, you can promote the sale of your home. It's something to consider.

Selling Checklist

1. Price: Is it right?_____
2. Location: Is there anything you can do to improve it? _____
3. Exposure: Have you got your agent cracking? _____
4. Appearance: Is it time for more paint? _____
5. Time: Have you waited long enough? _____

2

14 Days to Shaping Up Your House for Sale

Fixing up and cleaning up your home is a big part of selling it. While you may be satisfied with the way your property looks on a day-to-day basis, in order to get top dollar and a quick sale, you'll certainly want to put it into tip-top shape.

But what should you do? And how will you find the time to do it?

Here's a 2-week home shape-up plan that anyone should be able to handle. You can do the work yourself (in the evenings and on weekends). Or you can hire someone to do it. Either way, it will end up making your home far more presentable to potential buyers.

Day 1: Trim the Hedges

There are two purposes for this. The first is to cut back on all that growth that's accumulated over the years so that buyers can see your house more easily. After all, they're presumably interested in purchasing a home, not a forest.

The second is to get you ready for Day 2, which calls for painting the front of your home. If you've trimmed back the hedges, it makes it that much easier to get in there and paint.

Day 2: Paint the Front

Unless you've had your home painted within the past year, it's going to need some work in the front. Forget about "touching it up." After a year of exposure to the sun, the paint will have faded to the point where attempting to spot-paint any area where there has been discoloration, flaking, peeling, and so on will only end up giving your home a blotched look. Bite the bullet and paint it. It will make the front of your home look terrific in terms of "curb appeal," that all-important first impression.

TIP—MAXIMIZE YOUR HOME'S CURB APPEAL

We've all heard the adage, "You never have a second chance to make a good first impression." The point is well taken. Attitudes toward people and homes are usually fixed and sometimes unchangeable after that first glance. With regard to homes, that first impression is called *curb appeal*. It means how well your home shows itself off when that potential buyer drives up the very first time. That's why painting and polishing up the front of your home is so important.

Choose your colors carefully. They should blend in well with the other houses in the neighborhood. If your home is more than 10 years old, be especially careful about simply repainting using the original colors. Color trends change, and what was modern and fresh-looking a decade ago probably looks stale and old-fashioned today.

Check with a color expert (typically found at a good paint store). Such a person should be able to give you some useful suggestions. Also, check with any homeowners' association you may have to find out about any restrictions on paint colors. You may also want to check with your local building or planning department regarding paint color restrictions in your home's CC&Rs (Conditions, Covenants, and Restrictions that run with the land).

Day 3: Paint the Trim

If you began trimming the hedges on a Friday, you can spend the weekend painting the front and the trim of your home. Allow 2 days for the painting. Even with fast-drying water-based paints, you'll want to do the trim on the second day, lest it bleed into the wall paint.

Select a good complementary color for the trim. Again, paint stores have excellent color charts that show you which trim colors go best with which basic colors. While you'll certainly want to select a neutral color that will appeal to (or at least not offend) most buyers, you may also want to be just a little bit rakish so that your house will stand out from its neighbors. (See the discussion for Day 2 about homeowners' associations and CC&Rs.)

Day 4: Mow the Lawn, Clean the Driveway, Polish the Brass

These are things that you can easily do yourself. You'll have to keep the lawn and front looking good during the sales period, however, so hiring a gardener, even on a temporary basis, may make a lot of sense.

TIP—CONSIDER THE MARKET YOU'RE IN

In a hot market, buyers tend to overlook more about a house's condition. Yes, if it's in terrible shape, they will knock the price down. But if it's in "okay" shape, chances are that they won't complain that much. In a hot market, it's hard enough for buyers to just find a house to buy in a price range they can afford, let alone worrying about the small stuff.

Driveway cleaning can come down to putting a new coat of tar on an asphalt driveway or using cleaners to remove stains from a cement driveway. If the driveway is seriously cracked, however, you should consider more extensive repair work.

By the way, sometimes it's much easier to replace the door handles and other brasswork on the front of the house than to polish them up.

Day 5: Evaluate and Remove Furniture

What you see as "cozy" most buyers will see as cluttered. Get a real estate agent to come in and help you evaluate your clutter. Most of them can quickly tell you what to clean out in order to make your house look more open and friendly.

Then get rid of that excess furniture. Store it, sell it, or dump it. If you do so, buyers will think your home is just right.

When you're thinning out your furniture, here's a list of things you should get rid of to help you along.

Clutter Removal Checklist

- Extra furniture. One double or queen in a bedroom is the maximum. One table and set of chairs in a dining room. No cluttered chairs or couches in living room or family room. No rugs on top of rugs.
- Any clothes that are not in drawers or *neatly* hung in closets.
- Any toys that are scattered on the floor and not neatly put away in drawers or boxes.
- Any items that would get in the way of a buyer's appreciation of the house.

Day 6: Paint the Kitchen

The kitchen is probably the single most important room of the house, in terms of buyers' perceptions. A modern, clean kitchen is a highlight. A dirty, old-fashioned kitchen will detract from a home's value.

The only way to really improve a kitchen is to fully renovate it, and this is something that you may want to consider if your kitchen is over 10 years old.

However, major kitchen renovations can be very expensive, with costs today running from a low of around $10,000 to a high of $75,000 or more. Furthermore, they take time—anywhere from 1 to 6 months. Hence, they are beyond the scope of this book. If you are thinking about a major kitchen renovation, be sure you check out the cost/benefit of doing so. It may turn out that it will cost you more to do the work than you can back in return.

For shaping up your house to get a quick sale, however, you can easily and inexpensively paint the walls and ceiling of your kitchen. (In some cases, when older cabinets are in good physical shape, they too can be painted or restained.) The fresh coat of paint, particularly if it's white or a very light color, will freshen your kitchen no matter what the condition of the cabinets, countertop, and appliances. (Be sure that these are thoroughly cleaned so that they, too, offer the best possible appearance.)

Day 7: Clean or Replace the Kitchen Floor

It should go without saying that you'll want to clean the kitchen floor. However, if your home is 25 years old or older and has the original kitchen flooring, you may find that it's a darker color: yellow, green, or red. This was considered fashionable back then.

Today, however, kitchen floors tend to be either very light or very dark (black). The flooring of your kitchen may severely date it.

While replacing cabinets, countertops, and appliances can be costly and time-consuming, you can usually have your kitchen floor replaced with modern linoleum in a single day. Like painting, this will immensely improve your kitchen's appearance and, if you choose carefully, won't cost you an arm or a leg. It's something to consider.

Day 8: Paint the Guest Bathroom

Bathrooms are small. But just because they don't take up a lot of room doesn't mean that they are easy to paint. Actually, their small size makes them more difficult.

The guest bathroom is something that buyers will always check. While doing a full renovation (replacing cabinets, tile, sink, tub, shower, and so on) is very costly, a simple repainting will often do a remarkable job of refreshing.

Be sure to choose light-colored glossy paints. Allow a full day for this.

Day 9: Paint the Master Bathroom

Like the guest bathroom, the master bathroom is something that is important to buyers. Take a second day to paint it. (Be sure not to get any paint on the fixtures or the floor!)

Day 10: Paint (or Clean) the Entry and the Living Areas

Be judicious here. Go through the house and look at the walls in the living areas. Are they scratched? Do they have marks? Do they look tired and worn?

If so, clean them up. If you've repainted in the previous 6 months, you may be able to clean them. Otherwise, plan on painting them.

If the walls are already a light and neutral color, try using the same color. It will make repainting far easier.

TIP—YOU USUALLY DON'T NEED TO PAINT THE CEILING

Usually ceilings remain clean. Therefore, you need to repaint only the walls. Just be very careful not to get any paint from the walls onto the ceiling; if you do, you'll have to paint the ceiling too.

Day 11: Paint (or Clean) the Bedrooms

The same rule that applied to the living areas applies here. You don't want to see marks, gashes, or scratches, and the easiest way to remove these is to repaint.

TRAP—IT'S OFTEN EASIER TO PAINT THAN TO CLEAN

 Cleaning a spot on a wall seems a whole lot easier than painting the whole wall. However, when you clean a spot, you often only succeed in making the wall look worse. The reason is that the entire wall gets dirty, and a cleaned area (assuming that you can get the spot off) makes the rest of the wall look bad. Simply repainting the entire wall is usually easier.

If you're doing the painting yourself, be sure to remove as much furniture as possible. And use copious drop cloths to protect the furniture that you can't move.

Day 12: Wash the Windows, Clean the Lights

Dirty windows suggest a dirty house. And buyers always look out of (or sometimes into) the windows. If you don't do windows, hire someone who does. It won't cost much, and it will make a big difference.

Also, clean all light fixtures. These accumulate lots of dirt and dead bugs over time. Cleaning them will increase their brightness and make your house look cheery.

You may want to replace the existing light fixtures with brighter, more modern ones. This can be costly, but it can quickly add a modern touch to your home.

Day 13: Clean, Trim, Mow, and Plant Flowers in the Backyard

You don't need the Palace of Versailles in your backyard. But, the backyard should be neat and trim. And lots of fresh, blooming flowers help to make it look more livable. These can be purchased for very little and usually planted with ease. (Also do the same for your side yards.)

If you have a patio, make sure it's free of clutter. A nice table and chairs help—toys, boxes, and other junk scattered around do not. If you don't have a patio, don't worry about it. It shouldn't detract that much from your home. Just be sure that your lawn (if you have one) is well trimmed, and put some lawn furniture on it.

Day 14: Have the Carpet Cleaned (or Replaced)

This is very important, since most people look down as they walk through a home. If the carpet is clean and in good shape, they will figure that the entire home is the same way. If the carpet is worn and covered with dirt spots, their assumption about the house will be more negative.

If you have a relatively new carpet (less than 3 years old), cleaning may be all that is required. On the other hand, if your carpet is worn and very dirty, consider replacing it. Even inexpensive new carpeting looks terrific. You can get a whole house (around 2000 square feet) recarpeted for around $3000 to $4000 if you select one of the new Olephin carpets. (They won't hold up as long as nylon, but their initial appearance is wonderful.) And you might add this much and more to what you will get for your home in return, not to mention getting a quicker sale.

Do the carpeting last. That way you won't have to worry about spilling any paint on it.

Remember, First Impressions Count

If the would-be buyer's first impression is positive, then he or she will walk through your home looking for reasons to seal the deal. If it's negative, that person will go through your home looking for reasons to avoid buying your property. You want to accent the positive and avoid the negative.

Following through on this 14-day shape-up will help guarantee that your house will make a good first impression.

After the 14-Day Shape-Up

Beyond the 14-day shape-up, if your home is already in pretty good shape, you probably can get by with little additional fix-up work. However, be sure that what you see as "pretty good shape" is what a potential buyer will also see as "pretty good shape."

Pretty good shape usually means that the paint on the outside looks good all over, not just in the front (no blisters, peeling, or fading) and the paint on the inside has no marks or scratches. It means that the lawns around the property don't have bald spots and aren't overgrown with weeds, and that the house has hedges and trees and decent landscaping everywhere.

It means that all the appliances work and the entire house is neat, clean, and presentable. (If you've lived in your present home for more than 6 months, chances are that you've got a couple of loads of trash and throwaways stashed here and there that you would do well to throw away.)

TIP—KEEP YOUR KITCHEN READY TO SHOW

Never, never leave dirty dishes out. Nothing turns buyers off more.

What If My Home Is in Bad Shape?

Now you have to make the decision whether it's worth it to do major renovation work. Keep in mind that if you don't do needed repair work, buyers will begin characterizing your property as a "fixer-upper" and will submit lowball offers. Buyers always exaggerate the cost of fixing up a property. On the other hand, when it comes to major renovation, we're talking serious money—possibly tens of thousands of dollars.

TRAP—IT MAY COST MORE TO DO NOTHING

You should do a cost/reward analysis. How much will it cost to do the renovation work you are considering? How much will it add to the value of your home? If it adds more value than it costs, borrow the money and do the work. If it doesn't, consider doing less work. Also, take into consideration the time needed to find a buyer. Sometimes doing the renovation will mean a much quicker sale.

The following list describes the most common major renovations, along with tips on how to handle them.

Most Common Renovation Work

1. *Roof.* Sometimes you can simply fix the leaks in an old roof rather than replacing it. The cost is far, far less.

2. *Insulation.* Older homes do not have much insulation, but today's buyers are keen on energy efficiency and will sometimes turn down a property just because it lacks adequate insulation. The cost of adding blown-in insulation to an attic is low. Adding insulation to walls on an already constructed house, however, is enormously costly and should be avoided if at all possible.

3. *Electrical and plumbing systems.* You'll need to bring the electricity and pipes up to minimal safety standards in any event. In most cases, the amount of work needed is minimal. On the other hand, if you have to convert galvanized steel pipes to copper pipes, be prepared for a major blow to your wallet.

4. *Walls.* External stucco should be patched, unless it's so badly broken up that it has to be totally replaced. Patching is cheap; replacement is very expensive. Interior wallboard should be patched where there are holes. You can do this yourself for next to nothing. (See instructions at home building stores.)

5. *Garage door.* New hinges and springs are a good idea for safety reasons and are inexpensive. Most wooden doors can be repaired inexpensively. Metal doors may have to be replaced if dented.

6. *Landscaping.* If you put in a new lawn by sod, it costs more, but it is instantly green. Seeds take up to 3 months to produce lush grass but cost pennies per square foot. Forget about adding shade trees. They need years to grow, and planting trees that are already large is costly. Flower beds, however, are inexpensive and add color and vitality to landscaping. Also, fix the fence if it's falling down. Buyers start adding up costs when they see a broken fence.

7. *Built-in appliances.* Broken appliances should be fixed or replaced. Sometimes it's cheaper to replace them than to fix them. For example, an entire electric range and oven may cost under $400, whereas a single burner (there are usually five to seven on the unit, including the oven) could cost $150.

There could, of course, be other areas that require major repair. In all cases, you should get bids and also competitively price the materials yourself to determine whether you'll get the money that you put into repair work out of the sale and/or whether doing the repair work will help you sell faster.

What If My Property Is a Real Dog?

Many people have never seen a house that is in truly terrible condition. Typically this occurs when absentee owners rent the place out to tenants who just don't care. For many readers, the following list will just make them feel good about their own property. Here are some things that could be wrong with a property that would make your hair stand on end.

Problems with a House in Terrible Condition

Appliances—ripped apart, stolen, or smashed

Bathroom fixtures—ripped off walls or out of floors and broken

Light fixtures—stolen or smashed (including the electrical receptacle)

Windows—broken

Doors—broken

Screens—gone

Plumbing—broken lines

Electrical—main circuit box smashed, circuit breakers broken, wiring pulled out

Walls and ceiling—major holes

Yard—no landscaping; weeds, rocks, and dirt

Fences—broken

Exterior—stucco falling apart, wood torn off or broken, metal siding bent or broken loose

Ridiculous, you may say? A house could never get that bad? I've seen them that bad and worse. But just because it's in terrible shape doesn't mean that the house is valueless. It just means that you have to decide on a plan of action.

You have several choices:

1. Fix it up completely.
2. Fix it up for safety and cosmetic effect.
3. Let it alone and sell it as a fixer-upper for much less.

At this point you have to realize that buyers ordinarily suffer from an appalling lack of imagination. If you have a house that is a real dog and you're fortunate enough to get a buyer to walk into the front door, chances are 99 out of 100 that the buyer will immediately turn around and walk out. The vast majority of buyers, even many investor buyers, won't want to fool around with a real dog.

That means that in order to sell the property, you're probably going to have to do *some* work. You'll have to fix it up, either totally or just cosmetically (enough to sell).

TIP—FINANCE THE RENOVATION

It can cost big bucks to fix up a house, so you should consider short-term financing in the form of a homeowner's loan or a home equity loan. In many cases, the interest on such a loan is tax-deductible, as are *many* of your fix-up expenses. Check with your accountant.

Should You Fix Up a Dog of a House?

You simply have to do a cost/reward analysis. In a strong market and in a good area, the answer is undoubtedly yes. However, in a bad market and in a terrible neighborhood, maybe the best you can do is slap some paint on and hope for the best.

Do I Have the Energy?

Then, there's the matter of how much energy you are willing (or have) to devote to the fix-up. Some of us are natural putterers. For them, fixing up a place is fun.

For most of the rest of us, however, fun is playing golf, watching TV, or reading a good book. And then there are those who have two left hands and wouldn't think of trying to do the fix-up themselves.

Where do you fit in? (It's important that you know, because if you have to hire people to do everything, it could be prohibitively expensive.)

Here's my suggestion: If you don't want to (or can't) spend a lot of energy yourself fixing up your home before you sell, forget it. Pay someone else to do what's minimally necessary to cosmetically clean and paint your property. Then take the lower price and wait the longer time to find a buyer. (Sometimes it's more important to cater to yourself than to cater to your house.)

On the other hand, if you're a bundle of energy, then by all means leap into the fray and fix up your house yourself. Try to do much of the work yourself, since that's actually the best way to save money.

TRAP—DON'T OVERDO IT

Many sellers fall into the trap of thinking that by doing *excessive* fix-up work on their house, they can make *even more* money from the sale. Chances are that just isn't so. Your property will have a top market value beyond which it just won't go at the present time. What you are doing when you fix it up is trying to present it in such a way that you get that top dollar. You do the *minimal amount of fix-up possible*. Any additional fixing could turn your property into a white elephant, overbuilt for its neighborhood.

14-Day Home Shape-Up Checklist

Day 1: Trim the Hedges	[ ]
Day 2: Paint the Front	[ ]
Day 3: Paint the Trim	[ ]
Day 4: Mow the Lawn, Clean the Driveway, Polish the Brass	[ ]
Day 5: Evaluate and Remove Furniture	[ ]
Day 6: Paint the Kitchen	[ ]
Day 7: Clean or Replace the Kitchen Floor	[ ]
Day 8: Paint the Guest Bathroom	[ ]
Day 9: Paint the Master Bathroom	[ ]
Day 10: Paint (or Clean) the Entry and the Living Areas	[ ]
Day 11: Paint (or Clean) the Bedrooms	[ ]
Day 12: Wash the Windows, Clean the Lights	[ ]
Day 13: Clean, Trim, Mow, and Plant Flowers in the Back Yard	[ ]
Day 14: Have the Carpet Cleaned (or Replaced)	[ ]

For more information on this subject, check into the *Home Renovation Checklist* (McGraw-Hill, 2003).

3
Pricing to Hook Buyers

What is the single most attractive feature of your home?

Is it the front entrance? The fireplace? A lovely master bedroom suite? Maybe it's a redone kitchen?

All of these features can attract a buyer. But nothing will be more attractive, more like honey to a bee, than an attractive price. The price makes all the difference. Place your home on the market for even a few thousand dollars more than buyers perceive it's worth, and it may languish without offers, even in a hot market. On the other hand, price it just a few thousand below what buyers perceive as its value, and it can sell quickly, even in a stone-cold market.

Of course, any given home will have a *range* of prices. You will want your home to be in top shape (see the previous chapter) so that you will be able to get a price at the top of the range.

What Is the Right Price for Your Home?

For practical purposes, the price for almost any home is determined solely by the marketplace. If a home in a given neighborhood sells for $250,000, then presumably another identical home in the same neighborhood is also worth $250,000. Thus, if you then price the second home at $260,000, you're putting it "above market," and that will keep buyers away. On the other hand, if you price it at $240,000, you're putting it "below market," and that will attract buyers.

Thus the fastest way to sell your home is to price it slightly under market. The slowest way to sell your home is to price it even just a little bit above market.

TIP—BUYERS ARE VERY PRICE-SENSITIVE

Years ago, when homes sold for far, far less, buyers tended to overlook a price that was just a little bit above market. After all, we were then talking about perhaps only a few hundred dollars on a $25,000 home. Today, however, a $300,000 home that's only 2 percent over market is $6000 too high. That's something that catches a buyer's attention.

Of course, in real life, pricing isn't quite that precise. Rather than there being one identical comparable home, there are often several similar homes that have sold at different prices. It's your job to find out what made the highest-priced home that valuable and see if you can't make your home similarly valued. On the other hand, if you don't do anything to fix up your house, you can expect to get the bottom of the price range.

All of which is to say that this chapter is a pitch to get you to price your home correctly. Price it at market (or just below), or at what buyers perceive to be its true value, and you'll quickly get a sale. Price it too high, and you'll sit and wait, and get frustrated, and keep making payments, and not be able to move. (Price it too low, of course, and you'll lose money!)

So, how do you find that magic number that is just the right price for your home?

For one thing, be realistic. Remember the cardinal rule of marketing your home.

CARDINAL RULE OF MARKETING A HOME

The market price for your home is determined by buyers.

Most of us think that the seller sets the price for the home. Nothing could be further from the truth. It's buyers who set the price. The seller can either go along with that price and sell or not go along with it and keep the house.

Always keep the following factors in mind.

What Does *Not* Determine Market Price

1. *Not* how much you paid for the home

2. *Not* how much you owe on the home

3. *Not* how high (or low) your taxes are

4. *Not* how much you put into the home (in improvements)

5. *Not* how much you love the home

What determines the price, quite simply, is what a buyer is ready, willing, and able to pay. (That also, by the way, is what your agent will say when he or she demands a commission—that he or she has brought you a buyer who is ready, willing, and able to purchase.)

So, how do we know what a buyer will be ready, willing, and able to pay? The answer is that we check to see what previous buyers have paid for similar homes. Determining price usually comes down to comparisons. How does the unknown quantity, in this case your home, stack up against the known quantity, other similar homes that have already sold?

TRAP—NO TWO HOMES ARE IDENTICAL

The word *similar* is most appropriate. No two homes are ever truly identical, and even if they are both in the same neighborhood, their locations are almost never exactly equal. (One may be on a busier street, the other closer to a park, and so on.)

Thus determining price becomes as much judgment as science.

How Do I Find "Comparables"?

How do you find comparable homes and learn the prices they sold for? Ask an agent.

However, before you start, I have a working suggestion for you: Open your mind. Put aside all previous perceptions, suppositions, and dreams about what your home is worth. You may have been at a garden party where your neighbors, as they tend to do, were talking real estate. They were commenting on how a house up the street (just like everyone else's in the neighborhood) recently sold for $450,000. Wow, everyone goes, adding an extra "0" to the value of their property. Forget it. The time for guessing is gone. Now, it's time to find out which homes are true comparables.

TIP—THINK LIKE A BUYER

Become a pretend buyer for a weekend to quickly gain a better knowledge of the housing market in your area. Go around with a broker (or by yourself to open houses) and see what's out there. It won't take you very long at all to begin sizing up the market.

The one most important thing that every real estate agent learns is the market. No agent worth her or his salt is ignorant about homes and their prices. Therefore, why not tap into that readily available knowledge? I'm not suggesting that you call a broker to list your house—at least, not yet. I'm just suggesting that you contact an agent for information.

Remember, agents are anxious to please you. They hope that if they help you in every way they can, when you finally do decide to list, you'll give them the listing. Take advantage of their generosity. (And you may discover an agent with whom you'd like to list!)

Here's what to tell the agent: "I'm thinking of putting my house up for sale. I want to ask a competitive price. Can you supply me with a list of *comparables* for my home?" What you are asking for is a list of homes similar to yours that have recently been sold and the sale prices (and original listing prices) for those homes. If you just compare the houses on this list with your home, you'll almost instantly have a good idea of the market range.

Providing you with such a list is the easiest of things for an agent to do. Virtually all areas of the country have listing services (such as the Multiple Listing Service [MLS]), and nearly all agents belong to them. Today these listing services are computerized, and their databanks can provide members with all kinds of lists, including those for sales and houses currently for sale going back months and sometimes years.

These lists can be chosen by neighborhood, by price, by type of house, and so on. On most services, the agent, with the tap of a few buttons on a computer, can print out a list of comparable homes sold in your section of town, your neighborhood, even your street.

Do It Yourself on the Web

If you don't want to deal with an agent at this stage of the game, simply go on the Web and check into one of the many sites that provide comparables. The chances are excellent that you'll find not only your neighborhood, but even your own house there!

For a fee of only a few dollars, you can quickly and usually reliably be supplied not only with a list of comparables, but with their listing and sales prices and their features, so that you can check to see if they really are similar to yours.

To get to such services, check the Resources section at the end of the book.

How Do I Analyze Comparables?

Once you have a list of comparables, you must analyze that list. That means that you must make a judgment call about which of the homes that have recently been sold are truly similar to yours and which are not.

Okay, you've got a list of six or so homes that you believe are comparable to yours. But are they really? Maybe they're all painted purple, have terrible landscaping, or are on awkward-shaped lots on heavily trafficked streets. Maybe they aren't at all like your home; maybe their condition and location within the neighborhood makes them much worse—or much better!

TRAP—BE CURRENT

 The real estate market is constantly in a state of flux. Prices that are more than 6 months old are often out of date. Your house could be worth considerably more—or considerably less—than old prices suggest.

Check them out.

It won't take you that long to drive by them, and with just a glance you can upgrade or downgrade them in terms of how comparable their neighborhood (location) and outside appearance are to yours. Don't skip this important step.

Next, compare the rest of the home. Again, this is really a judgment call; however, you can ask your agent (and sometimes your neighbors and friends who might have seen the sold home) to help you make it. Is your home in better shape than the comps? (The old listings will often indicate if the comp was a dog—look for clues such as "needs TLC" or "a handyman special.") Does it have more or fewer amenities (a pool, spa, extra large garage, and so on) than yours? Was it larger (in terms of square feet) or smaller than yours?

You'll need to make these comparisons and raise or lower your price accordingly. This is called adjusting your home to its price range. Of course, you'll want to be at the top of the range. On the other hand, you'll also need to be realistic. Again, a good agent can be invaluable in helping you with this.

Do the Numbers

Once you've developed a range for your home, it's time to do a number comparison.

Step 1: Do a Gross Analysis

When you get the list of comparables, first check to see if there is one sale on the list that seems suspiciously low compared with the others or one that seems suspiciously high. I don't mean to automatically throw out the highest and lowest. Just be suspicious of them. Perhaps there was something unusual about the sale (which you may never know about). Perhaps the seller was divorcing and had to take the first offer, no matter how low, or perhaps the buyer fell in love with the property and paid far too much for it. Just eliminate the odd fellow, the property or situation that isn't like yours.

Also, beware of being too optimistic. Most sellers looking at a list of comparables automatically let their eyes fall on the highest-priced home there and figure that's what their own home is worth. It's only natural to think that your property is worth top dollar. But will buyers really see it that way?

Step 2: Compare List to Sales Price

Many times the inventory of homes you receive will include both sales and list prices. The list prices of homes that are currently on the market can be deceptive. Most of the homes that are currently for sale will *not* sell for their listed price. They will sell for less. (Unless it's an overheated market, when they may actually sell for more!) Eventually the sellers will get desperate and reduce their price, or, if they insist on an unrealistic value, they may simply take their home off the market.

List price is what the seller is asking. Rarely, except in very hot markets, does the seller get that amount. To look only at the asking prices of houses that are currently listed can give you a false sense of value.

On the other hand, knowing list price can be very useful. After all, since buyers typically offer less than list, you will want to price your home higher than your hoped for sales price. Checking the list prices will clue you in as to how much higher to go.

Try to do a comparison of at least six homes. Write down both their listed and their sales prices. Now take your calculator and do a little math. Divide the *sales price into the differences between sales and list price* for those half-dozen homes. This will give you the percentage difference between the asking (list) price and the sales price.

TIP—KNOW THE DIFFERENCE BETWEEN LIST AND SALES PRICES

Knowing the percentage difference between list and sales prices tells you how active the market is as well as how much less than your asking price you can expect to sell your home for. (It will tell you, in effect, the market's condition.)

The table shown here provides an example to help you learn how to analyze the difference between the listing price and the sales price.

List versus Sales Price Comparison Example

List Price	Sales Price	Difference
$114,000	$109,000	–5
$120,000	$108,000	–12
$115,000	$107,000	–6
$116,000	$110,000	–6
$112,000	$109,000	–3
$105,000	$107,000	–2

Note that although the list prices have a $15,000 range (from $105,000 to $120,000), the sales prices have only a $3000 range (from $107,000 to $110,000). In other words, although sellers asked more, buyers have determined that the homes are worth between $107,000 and $110,000.

Note also that in all but one case, the price at which the sold homes were listed was within 5 percent of the sales price. In only one case did a severely overpriced home actually sell. Again, remember that buyers are price-sensitive. Price your home too high, and it will seldom get a buyer.

Also note that in one case, a home that was priced too low sold for more than the list price, probably because of multiple offers. Finally, notice again that 5 percent difference between list and sales prices— a common figure in most areas of the country in a stable market.

What Does the Percentage Difference Tell You?

The percentage difference between the list and sales prices tells you a number of things, including how realistic the asking prices for homes in the area are, how strong or weak the market is, and, indirectly, how long it may take to sell your home.

If the average percentage difference is less than 5 percent, you're in a healthy market. If your price is realistic, you'll get close to it, and it shouldn't take long to sell.

If the percentage differences are between 5 and 10 percent, you're in a soft market. Sellers aren't getting what they feel their homes are worth. Homes probably aren't selling quickly. To get a quick sale, you'll probably need to sell for much less than you've listed.

If the percentage differences are between 10 and 20 percent, the market is very weak. Few homes are selling—only those at fire-sale prices, probably picked up by speculators. You probably won't be able to sell your home for what you consider to be its true value in such a market.

Step 3: Check Out the Inventory and the Time Lag

The percentage difference between list and sales prices will also suggest the time lag, or how long it will take between listing and selling your home. Typically, the higher the percentage, the longer the time lag.

You can confirm this by asking your agent for data on the housing market inventory in your area.

Data to Get from Your Agent

- The number of homes currently for sale compared to the number available at the same time last year and the year before.

- How long the inventory will last. In an average market, there's sufficient inventory to last 6 months (it will take that long to sell all the houses). If the market is strong, the inventory will be down to 3 or even 2 months. If it's weak, the inventory will be up to 12 or even 18 months.

- How long it takes to close a sale. Short closing times (under 30 days) suggest a hot market. Long closing times and lots of deals falling out of escrow suggest a cold market.

**TRAP—YOU WON'T
GET DATA ON SALES
OF INDIVIDUAL
HOUSES BEFORE
CLOSING**

The agent probably won't be able to provide you with a list showing the prices sellers have accepted on sales that haven't yet closed. The reason is that if the current deal falls through, the seller would be at a disadvantage in that subsequent buyers would already know his or her best price. Since most agents represent sellers, they won't (or shouldn't) release this information.

Now, Set Your Home's Price

You have a list of six homes that are similar to yours. Should you ask the average sales price, the average list price, or the top or bottom price when you put your house up for sale?

My suggestion is that, when possible and depending on your own needs, you should ask *at a minimum* the average *list price.* If you ask the average list price, you can expect to get the average sales price.

Remember, however, that in reality average list and sales prices are only indicators, clues, hints. Your house may be much better (or worse) than the average, and you may be able to ask and get more (or less) because of its condition. However, it's unlikely that you'll get more than the highest price that a house on your list recently sold for. Move out of your price range, and you've created a white elephant, a house that's priced too high for its neighborhood.

TRAP—DON'T LIST FOR TOO LITTLE

Don't make the mistake of listing your home for the average sales price. Except in a hot market, buyers don't offer list price; they tend to offer less. Thus, *no matter what price you ask,* you'll tend to get lower offers. Ask too little and you could end up selling your home for less than it's worth. To get the average sales price, you normally have to ask the average list price. (Beware of agents who encourage you to list for less hoping to encourage lots of activity. Sometimes it results in a bidding war that's to your advantage. Other times, it can result in your getting less than you want for your home.)

TIP—ANTICIPATE THE MARKET

If the market is going up, increase your price. For example, suppose the market is going up 10 percent a year in your area. The last home sold 3 months ago. Chances are that since it sold, the market has gone up 2.5 percent (¼ of a year at 10 percent). After you find your ideal price, bump it up 2.5 percent so that you're keeping up with the market.

Pricing Decision Guide

Average sales price of comparables ------------->$_____

	Add	Subtract
	Add	Subtract
1. Better/worse neighborhood	$_____	$_____
2. Older/younger home	$_____	$_____
3. Better/worse condition	$_____	$_____
4. Other factors pro/con	$_____	$_____
Totals	$_____	$_____

Add/subtract for comparables --------------->+/–$_____

The true market price ----------------------->$_____

WHAT ABOUT "RANGE" PRICING?

In some areas of the country, agents have taken to listing homes for a range of prices rather than for a single price. For example, instead of listing for $295,000, they list the home between $280,000 and $310,000. They explain that this way buyers who are at the low end of the range are encouraged to make offers, while those at the high end will want to bid the highest price to be sure of getting the property.

From a seller's perspective, the advantage is that you hope to get a high-end offer. But, barring that, you tell potential buyers what your lowest acceptable price is so that, hopefully, you'll at least get that bottom price.

In a very hot market, this can work to your advantage, particularly when there are few homes in the inventory and lots of buyers competing. You can create a kind of "feeding frenzy" where buyers start low and then bid and overbid to get your home.

However, if the market suddenly turns cold, the inventory increases, or there is a perception that your home is simply not worth anywhere near your top price, you can expect to get lots of low-ball offers. Sometimes these will be for far less than the bottom of your price range.

Thus, range pricing is at best a gamble. In the right market it may help you sell for a higher price. However, in most markets it's more likely to get you a lower offer than simply setting a single price.

Is Your Price Right?

I can remember once going into a home that was owned by an elderly gentleman who had emphysema. He made it quite plain that the only real investment he had in the world was his house and that he wanted to sell it to me. He carefully explained that he had the following mortgages on the house:

First	$155,000
Second	15,000
Third	5,000
Fourth	6,000
Total	$181,000

He explained that he had so much indebtedness on the property because of his illness. He had borrowed to pay hospital bills. The third and fourth mortgages were actually liens put on his property by a doctor and a nursing home.

He then went on to explain that he needed to get $50,000 cash out of his house. He needed that to pay for his continuing medical treatment. If I could find someone to give him that amount of money, he would sign in a minute.

I had already checked comparables, the neighborhood, and the condition of his house. In my opinion, it wasn't worth more than $185,000, tops. He really didn't even have enough equity to pay his normal closing costs, let alone realize $50,000 cash from the sale.

I didn't see how he could get any cash at all out.

As gently as I could, I tried to explain the *realities* of the situation to him. He listened patiently until I was finished and then said, "That's all well and good. But I still need to get $50,000 out of the sale!"

The point here is that no matter how urgent your need, what you want to sell your home for is irrelevant when it comes time to sell. The sales price is determined by what a buyer who is ready, willing, and able will pay for the property. The fact that you have mortgaged your home for more than that amount or that you want a specific amount of cash out just doesn't matter.

It's a shame, it's sometimes sad, but it's the facts as they are. As Jesse Livermore (who made $22 million in stocks during the Depression, then lost $20 million of it in commodities) once said, "There ain't no money lying on the streets, and if there was, ain't nobody shoveling it into your pocket." The market ultimately determines the highest sales price you will be able to get for your house.

Can You Live with the Right Market Price?

At the beginning of this chapter, you were asked to become a pretend buyer for a weekend and look at the market. For readers who did that, I'm sure it was an education in itself. After visiting an agent and getting sales and list prices, you should have an even better idea of the market. Finally, after going through this guide, you should have a dollar amount that expresses what you can realistically get for your home.

Is this a figure that you can live with? If you sell for that price, will you net out what you need to buy your next home or pay your other expenses?

Or is it so far out of bounds in terms of what you want and need that you're ready to throw up your hands in frustration?

If you can't live with the realistic price, I suggest you read Chapters 9 through 11. They give suggestions about alternatives to selling through an agent, including renting out your home for a time and selling by owner.

TRAP—DON'T GET SIDETRACKED BY OTHER PRICING SCHEMES

There are a variety of other methods (besides looking at comparables) for analyzing the value of property. For example, the *cost approach* determines value by the cost of rebuilding. The *income approach* determines value by the potential rental income of the house. Forget such methods. They are great for brand-new homes or income-producing investment property. But for residential resales, there is only one realistic approach, and that is to check comparables as discussed here. The comparable method is not only the approach preferred by competent appraisers but the one that lenders almost entirely rely upon.

What about Getting an Appraiser?

You've done your homework, and you have an excellent idea of what your house is worth. But you're still not sure. You would like the stamp of approval of a professional. It's time to call in an appraiser.

You can get an appraiser to give you a qualified *opinion* as to the value of your house. The cost is usually around $350. Look for an appraiser in the phone book under that heading.

Find an appraiser who has either an MAI or an SREA designation. A good mortgage broker can also suggest an appraiser. However, keep in mind that in a low-interest-rate market, appraisers are typically very busy handling lots of refinances. It may be some time before you can get one out to your home.

A professional appraiser should give you a written opinion of your house's value. It will undoubtedly take into account comparables, and it may perhaps also use the cost and income approaches, as if the property were new or a rental. Of course, the bottom line is that the appraisal will give you, presumably, one figure—the value of your home. See how it compares with the figure you arrived at by checking comparables on your own.

You can also get a broker to give you an opinion as to the value of your home. Most brokers will do this for free in the hopes of eventually getting a listing out of you. (Of course, you need not list just to get an appraisal.)

TRAP—GET IT IN WRITING!

If you want to have a broker appraise your property, make sure that he or she gives you a *written* appraisal and that it is understood up front that there will be no charge. Some agents will want to bill you for several hundred dollars for the work. The trouble is that these are not professional appraisers. Beware of them. Be sure you have it in writing either that the appraisal is free or, if there is a charge, what that charge is and your agreement to it. (Quite frankly, I would not normally pay for any appraisal given by a real estate agent—or anyone else—who was not a professional appraiser.)

Most brokers who are willing to give you an appraisal just use the comparables approach described in this chapter. Typically, even before they come out to meet you, they've looked up your neighborhood and evaluated comparables for your size home. Once they're at your house, they just check its condition and mentally knock off a few dollars or add a few on.

You may be asking yourself, "If an agent can give me an appraisal in just a few minutes, why should I bother going to all the trouble of doing it myself?" The answer is confidence. Your own appraisal has one big advantage: You can totally trust yourself. You know the work you did and the effort you put forth.

Yes, it's nice to see that an appraiser and an agent roughly agree with you. (If they don't, you may want to check to see that you—or they—didn't make some gross error.) But if you do it yourself, you know how the price was arrived at. You're not worried that someone is trying to pull the wool over your eyes. That's really nice.

And later on, when an agent or buyer tries to knock the price down, you'll have the confidence to stick to your guns because you'll *know* what your house is really worth.

4

Finding a Really Good Agent

What makes a good agent? Most people will quickly say that a good agent is one who gets a quick sale!

While you certainly want to list with an agent who can get your home sold, you also want that agent to do other things for you as well.

Things a Good Agent Will Do

- Get the best price possible.
- Competently handle all the paperwork.
- Protect you throughout the deal (and afterwards).
- And not cost an arm and a leg!

If you consider those four requirements, you'll quickly come to the conclusion that the quality of the agent you choose is pretty important. A good agent will more than earn the money that he or she costs. A poor agent, while perhaps saving you money initially, can get you into more trouble than you'd ever imagine.

How Can I Find a Good Agent?

A good first step is to solicit recommendations. Ask your friends if they know people who have recently sold their home. There are so many agents around (close to 1 percent of the population in some areas) that almost everyone knows one. Did the sellers have a good experience? Ask them if they would use the agent again. Ask them if they have any reservations about the agent.

If you can't get a recommendation, then it's up to you to find an agent on your own. Finding any old agent is easy: Just put an FSBO (for sale by owner) sign on your front lawn. You'll have agents climbing all over you trying to get your listing. Finding a *good* agent, however, is a bit more difficult.

I don't recommend that you start out by putting a sign on your front lawn. Rather, pick a real estate office that's nearby (being close is important because, presumably, the agents will know the immediate area well) and check it out. Walk in and tell the receptionist or the salesperson who greets you that you want to talk to the broker. (Don't explain why, yet.)

Check Out a Nearby Real Estate Office

When the broker appears, explain that you are *thinking* of listing your house. You want to list with an office that's *active*. In fact, you'd like to list with the best salesperson (not lister) in the office.

But for now, you want to learn something about the office itself. For example, how many listings does the office currently have? If the office is active, the broker will be delighted to point out the many listings. If the office is a dud, there won't be many or any. Leave.

Be sure to ask for listings that were taken by the agents in this office. Don't be fooled if the broker takes out a book and shows you all the listings on the Multiple Listing Service (MLS). None of them may have been taken by that office.

Now ask how many of its *own listings* this office has sold in the past 6 months. The broker should know the exact number. If the agents haven't sold any, or if there's any hemming and hawing, leave.

Along the way, listen carefully to what the broker says. Is there one name, one agent, who keeps popping up? Is that agent, in fact, the best seller in the office?

At the end of your brief discussion, ask the broker who is the best seller in the office in terms of sales (not listings) made. Most brokers will chuckle at your audacity, but will also probably give you a straight answer. (Is it the same name that kept popping up in your earlier conversation?)

Get Personal

Now go see that person. Introduce yourself and ask not only how many properties he or she has sold, but also how many he or she has listed in the past 6 months. (You want to deal with a good salesperson, but also one who handles listings, not just the sales end of the business.)

Ask if you can have a list of the sellers of listings that this agent recently sold, with phone numbers. Explain that you'd like to call them to see what they thought of the service.

This is the acid test. Most sellers never ask to see such a list. They wouldn't think of it. After all, it sounds like you're asking to see something confidential.

It's not confidential. Sales of homes are all recorded and are all public knowledge. If you want to take the time to go down to the courthouse, you can compile your own list of recent sellers.

A strong agent, one who will work for you, will be *delighted* to give you a list of recent sellers. After all, what does the agent do but please clients? A weak agent will give you reasons why she or he can't give out the list. Leave.

TIP—KEEP YOUR EYES OPEN

In some offices, particularly the larger ones, the names of top agents, and in some cases even their pictures, are often posted on the walls. If you look carefully as you enter, your questions may be answered.

Interview Prospective Agents

While knowing that the agent is a great salesperson is an enormous plus for you, you also need to know something more about him or her. You want to be sure that the person is competent in the real estate business, is honest in her or his dealings, and is reliable.

You may want to ask the following questions to help you determine these things.

Agent Interview Questions

1. "How long have you been in the real estate business?" The learning curve for real estate is fairly long. The reason is that the

number of transactions a person can become involved with at any one time is limited. Usually it takes 3 to 5 years for an agent to have gotten a well-rounded education; 5 to 10 years is better.

2. "What professional organizations do you belong to?" The minimum here should be the local real estate board and Multiple Listing Service, as well as the state and National Association of Realtors® (NAR). The agent may also be a member of the chamber of commerce and local citizens' committees and have taken advanced courses through the NAR—all pluses.

3. "What will you do to expedite the sale of my home?" The answer here should be immediate, direct, and comprehensive. The agent should explain a plan of action that he or she hopes will sell your house. The plan should include:
    - Listing for a specified time. (Beware of agents who want to list for more than 3 months.)
    - Promotion, including talking up the listing at the local real estate board.
    - Advertising.
    - Open houses.

These, then, are some of the questions you can ask of your future agent. Here's a checklist to take with you when you interview an agent.

Agent Interview Checklist

1. Houses listed in the last 6 months.   _____

2. Houses sold in the last 6 months.   _____

3. References available?   _____

4. Agent fully licensed?   _____

5. Has been in the real estate business at least 3 to 5 years? _____

6. Belongs to many professional organizations?   _____

7. Offers a plan for selling my home?   _____

8. Does not ask for an overly long listing?   _____

Should I Go with a Chain or an Independent Office?

Twenty or thirty years ago, virtually all real estate agents were independent. Today, the majority belong to a national chain such as

Century 21, RE/MAX, Coldwell Banker, Prudential, or some other large company. These are big names and big companies.

Thus, one of the first questions that most sellers ask is: Should I go with a chain or with an independent?

The answer is that the question is often irrelevant. One of the best tips this book can give you is that you should go with the best agent you can find. If that agent happens to be associated with a chain, great. If the agent is independent, just as great.

Don't base your listing decision solely on the sign in front of the office. Here's why.

In all states, a real estate office must be operated by a broker licensed in that state. The licensed broker has the choice of hanging out a shingle with her or his name (or some other dba, or made-up name) on it or signing on to operate the office as a franchise of a national chain. (Recently, many of the national chains have begun operating their offices directly as wholly owned offices, not franchises.)

Many agents opt to work for the chain. The reason is usually survival. Let's take an example from the fast-food business. You drive into a town you've never been in before. You want something to eat. You want the meal to be fast and inexpensive, the premises to be clean and pleasant, and the food to be safe and at least minimally tasty.

How are you going to pick?

You could take your chances with the first diner that comes up. Or you could stop at a few stores and ask people their opinions. Or you could drive directly to McDonald's, Burger King, Wendy's, or the like.

The national fast-food chains all maintain standards, so that whether you go into a restaurant in Seattle or one in Orlando, you know you'll get the same quality of service and food. (One of the most surprising fast-food visits I ever made was to a jam-packed McDonald's on the Champs Elysées in Paris. The food was extraordinaire!)

A real estate chain affords the same name recognition and resulting business. Most real estate chains offer their agents advertising support, office management help, forms, and sometimes even colorful jackets in addition to their signs and logo. I know many real estate brokers who have doubled their income overnight by converting from being independent to belonging to a chain. In some cases, the only way they could stay in business was to join up. That's why so many choose to join.

The real question, of course, is what a chain offers *you*.

Pluses of Listing with a Chain

As just discussed, chains offer at least a minimal standard of performance. One office tends to look much like another, and in general the agents tend to be fairly well trained. In addition, chains offer long-distance moving assistance. List your home with a chain office in one city and an agent from a linked office in another city can already be looking for a new home for you.

In my opinion, the true value of the chain is that it brings a degree of order and homogeneity to real estate.

Pluses of the Independent Broker

On the other hand, there are the independents. They have limited advertising and name recognition. To make up for this, they usually have to work harder.

TIP—THEY'RE NOT NECESSARILY BETTER—THEY'RE JUST INDEPENDENT!

 Just because an office is independent, many people conclude that the agents have to be better in order to make it on their own. This isn't necessarily true. The agents could just as easily be so terrible that no chain would take them! On the other hand, a very good salesperson (or group of them) could be working for her- or himself and simply not want to give a percentage of each deal to the chain company.

What's important to understand is that where it counts, in selling, the independents can usually offer just as much as the chains. The reason is the listing services.

Usually both the independents and the chain offices belong to the same listing services (typically the MLS) in their area, and since nearly all houses are listed on these services, all agents, whether independent or in a chain, usually work on the same properties.

TRAP—SOME AGENTS
HOARD LISTINGS

That's not always the case. A recent trend has been for some large chains to hold some of their listings (typically the better ones) just for their agents.

However, competing listing services have recently begun popping up in large metropolitan areas. Thus, not every agent may be able to easily show you every listing. (However, if you want to see a particular house, your agent can call the lister, who will usually cooperate.)

Frequently Asked Questions on
Chains versus Independents

Won't the chain offer better service? The chain can offer name recognition, trained personnel, and usually more advertising. That doesn't necessarily translate into better service for you. Selling real estate remains a highly individualized operation. Remember, it's how much your lister pushes your property that counts.

Will the chain back up its salespeople's actions? That's a good question. Be sure to ask. Some do, at least minimally. Some don't. It depends on what the problem is.

What if an independent makes a mistake that costs me money? Today nearly all real estate agents carry errors and omissions insurance as well as some form of malpractice insurance. In addition, California and some other states maintain funds to at least partially compensate people who have been victimized by bad agents. Ask your independent what protections are offered.

It's important to understand that this discussion is not intended to knock or praise either chains or independents. I repeat, my advice is to go with the best agent you can find.

The Agent's Responsibility

If I agree to list, what does the agent owe me in return?

Listing your home for sale is not a one-way street. You agree to pay a hefty commission to the agent. But that agent also agrees to give you something in return.

The Agent Owes You

Service

Loyalty

Diligence

Honesty

Disclosure of facts

Skill

Care

Some of these may actually be stated in the listing agreement. Others are considered part of the agent's fiduciary responsibilities. All are considered examples of ethical conduct.

Buyers' Agents versus Sellers' Agents

When you list with an agent, he or she owes you loyalty. That takes many forms. The clearest expression of loyalty is when the agent brings you a sales agreement for $195,000, but tells you that she or he has overheard the buyers say that they would be willing to pay $200,000 for your house.

That little tidbit of information is worth $5000 to you. Without it, you might have accepted the $195,000 offer. With it, you hold out for $200,000—and get it.

Why should the agent be loyal to you and not to the buyer? Why should the agent give you this information that was worth so much money?

The Seller's Agent

The reason has to do with the agent's fiduciary (position of trust) relationship with you. It is incumbent upon the agent to tell you any fact that may help you in making your decision to sell.

It swings the other way, too. If you tell the agent that you would be willing to accept $195,000 when you're asking $200,000, but not to tell any buyers that fact, the agent is obligated to follow your wishes. In fact, because of the fiduciary relationship, the agent is prohibited (in theory) from telling the buyers anything about price or terms that you do not specifically tell the agent to divulge.

In other words, the agent is bound to you in ways that are definitely to your advantage.

TRAP—THE REAL
VERSUS THE IDEAL

 It's important not to get too smug about agency relationships. Not all agents stick to the letter of ethical conduct, and some agents (buyers' agents) may have fiduciary responsibilities to the buyers and not to you.

The Buyer's Agent

Thus far we've been talking about a seller's agent, the one who takes your listing. However, today many agents work for the buyer. They may even have the buyer sign an agreement like a listing.

Be wary of buyers' agents. They do not owe you the same fiduciary responsibility as do seller's agents. Indeed, their responsibilities are reversed. They owe the fiduciary responsibility to the buyers!

TIP—IT DOESN'T
MATTER WHO PAYS

 Whether an agent represents a buyer or a seller depends on whom the agent declares for. Who pays the agent is not the issue. In fact, it's common for the seller's (your) agent to split the commission with the buyer's agent, so, in effect, you're paying the buyer's agent!

What Are Subagents?

When you list your property with an agent, he or she owes you a fiduciary responsibility as described earlier. But what if the agent puts your property on the listing service and suddenly 100 or 1000 agents are all working it? Do they owe you a fiduciary responsibility?

Yes—and no.

If they act as *subagents* (meaning that your agent delegates agency powers to them), then they owe you the same duties and responsibilities.

However, some agents act independently, although they may still show your house and sell it off the listing service. These agents may work for the buyer. Or they may work for *both* you and the buyer.

What Are Dual Agents?

A dual agent is one who not only works for you, the seller, but also works for the buyer. The dual agent represents both parties. The crux of a dual agent's responsibilities can be found (just like the seller's agent's could) in giving information on the price. A dual agent should not tell a buyer that you're willing to take less *or tell you that the buyer is willing to pay more.*

In other words, the dual agent, because he or she owes both you and the buyer loyalty, usually forgoes disclosing price information (and other information, such as who's willing to concede terms) to either of you.

TIP—AGENTS MUST
OFFER DISCLOSURE

An agent must tell you whom he or she represents: you, the buyer, or both.

The National Association of Realtors offers a code of ethics that was the forerunner of many of the rules of agency in most states. The code of ethics basically requires that the agent deal fairly with all parties, both buyers and sellers.

Today, however, virtually all states require agents to disclose to you whom they represent. Thus, when you sign your listing agreement, the agent may also present you with a second document that gives, in effect, something like one of the following statements.

Typical Agents' Disclosure

Seller's agent: I am a seller's agent with the following duties and responsibilities to you . . . and I have a duty to disclose to you all facts affecting the value of the property.

Dual agent: I am a dual agent, and I represent both buyers and sellers. I might not disclose to you if a buyer is willing to pay more than the offered price.

Buyer's agent: I am a buyer's agent. I represent the buyer and owe that buyer a fiduciary responsibility, and I may not disclose to you if a buyer is willing to pay more than the offered price.

Usually you must not only read the disclosure, but sign to indicate that you understand what it says. (There's nothing wrong with signing—just be sure that you do, in fact, understand and agree to what the disclosure says.)

Which Type of Agent Do You Want?

Obviously, you're not going to want a buyer's agent. But what about a seller's agent versus a dual agent?

The answer should be straightforward: When you're selling your house, you want only a seller's agent. You want to be sure that the person with whom you list will represent you thoroughly.

That's all well and good. But what happens when your agent goes out and brings in a buyer (with no other agent involved)? Does your agent now become a *dual* agent?

Maybe. It all comes out in disclosure. The agent who brings you the offer on your house should disclose what type of agent she or he is. If the agent doesn't disclose, you should demand a disclosure.

Whenever an offer is presented, demand to know whom the agent presenting the offer represents. The agent should tell you. If the agent doesn't, presume that the agent is acting for the buyer and treat the offer adversarially. Keep a tight lip and don't blab what you might take, if it's less than what is being offered.

The point to understand here is that the agent determines whom she or he represents. Your goal is to find out who that is and then act accordingly. It all comes out in the wash when you ask your agent for advice such as, "Should I accept this offer?" You want to know which corner your agent is in when judging the answer.

Negotiating the Commission

Everything in real estate is negotiable, including the commission.

Once you've decided to list your home for sale and have found the right agent, it's time to negotiate the commission and the listing terms.

If this surprises you, you're not alone. Most first-time buyers and even a great many experienced ones aren't aware that commissions and listings are fully negotiable. They just assume that there's a going rate and that the agent will give them that rate.

Nothing could be further from the truth. There is no "going rate," and every agent will negotiate both the listing terms and conditions and the commission rate. Not every agent will necessarily accept what you may want to offer, but all agents should listen and consider it.

TIP—SOME AGENTS WON'T NEGOTIATE THE COMMISSION

If you find an agent who doesn't want to negotiate, listen carefully. Maybe, just maybe, the agent is so good that he or she can command a higher price. But before you list with such an agent, you'd better have some pretty solid indications that that agent can deliver a buyer at your price and terms in short order.

It is both illegal and unethical in all areas of the country for a real estate board to set a minimum commission rate. It's not done today. Lawsuits and judicial decisions have outlawed that practice. If an agent tells you that you must pay a "going rate" or a "set fee," find another agent.

Can I Knock Down an Agent's Commission?

In most cases, commission rates today for single-family residential property range from a low of 3 percent to a high of 7 percent. Let's say your agent walks in and says that she wants 7 percent. Should you pay it?

I had this happen to me several years ago when I was selling a house outside my area in a weak market. The agent pointed out that, yes, the commission was negotiable. However, she was an excellent salesperson, and her track record with sales of listings proved it. True, other offices in the area were asking only between 5 and 6 percent, but she was better than they were. Was I willing, she asked, to pay a lower rate and wait longer, perhaps forever, to sell my property? Wouldn't it be cheaper to pay a higher rate and get a quicker, sure sale?

I mention this example because the same type of argument may be used on you. Be aware, however, that it's most often the lister (an agent who only lists) who uses it.

I asked the agent if she would guarantee me a sale. She said she couldn't do that, but then again no one could. (*Note:* Some offices will guarantee to buy your home at a predetermined price if it doesn't sell within a set period of time. There could be inherent conflicts of interest here, as discussed later in this chapter.)

I asked if she could guarantee to sell my property faster than any other agent. She said she was sure she could sell it quickly. She couldn't guarantee that, but then again, nothing in this world had a guarantee attached to it.

I then asked her why, if she couldn't guarantee anything, she felt that she was entitled to a commission higher than those that other reputable, good agents were charging. She explained that it was because she was better than they, in her opinion, and would work harder for me.

I pointed out that each potential listing agent I talked with stressed that she or he was better than others, that all of them said that they would work hard for a quick sale, and that, as far as I could tell, she wasn't offering anything more for the additional rate. Then I showed her to the door.

The point here is that while there's nothing wrong with paying a higher price for better service, if it is better service. It's a shame to pay that higher price for standard service.

Aim Lower

There's no reason that you can't tell an agent what the maximum commission that you'll pay is. For example, you can say, "I'm willing to pay a 5 percent commission (or 4 percent or 2 percent, or whatever). Are you willing to work for that amount?" Now listen carefully to what the agent replies. Some will say that they can't afford to do a good job for that price, and then will decline and leave. That's probably an agent who knows what he or she is worth.

Others may say that, yes, they'll consider working for what you offer. However, they won't be able to perform all the normal tasks that go with selling. In return for a lower commission, they want you to do some of the work, such as showing the property or paying for some of the advertising.

Again, this is probably an agent who knows what it costs to sell a home and is offering you a way to share those costs.

Finally, others may say that, yes, they'll accept that commission rate and work just as hard as they would for a higher rate. I would be suspicious of these agents. They may also know what they're worth—and it could be a lot less than the other agents in terms of their ability to deliver a buyer who is ready, willing, and able to buy.

TRAP—BEWARE OF AGENTS WHO LOWBALL THE COMMISSION

Beware of agents who accept an unusually low commission. They may intend to simply list your house on a multiple listing service and let it go at that, with no additional support.

TIP—GO FOR THE ACTIVE AGENT

A good agent won't try to browbeat you into paying a higher commission. Good agents don't get rich by charging higher commissions or by making enemies of sellers. They get rich by making more deals.

While you don't want to try to "cheat" your agent into a low fee that will make him or her not want to serve you, you also don't want to pay an excessive fee. My suggestion is that you check with several agents to see what most of the agents in your area are charging and pay no more—and no less—than that.

Just because the commission is negotiable is not necessarily a good reason to insist on a low commission rate. You generally get what you pay for. Even though agents are ethically required to show the most appropriate homes to their buyers, in the real world, if you offer a lower commission than your next-door neighbor who has the same house at roughly the same price, which house do you think agents will be more likely to show?

Why Are Real Estate Commissions So High?

Even though the agent may make a good case for a 6 or 7 percent commission, one can't help but wonder why commissions in general are so high. For example, back in the 1950s, commissions were generally around 5 percent. By the 1990s, as several studies have shown, the average commission climbed to the 6 and sometimes 7 percent range.

In addition, back in the 1950s the average house cost only around $15,000. Today it's around $200,000. That means that back in 1950, an agent who sold a house for $15,000 at a 5 percent commission collected a total of only $750. Today an agent who sells a $200,000 house for 6 percent collects a whopping $12,000 commission.

Today's commission is over 15 times higher. Why?

There are three answers to this question.

Why Commissions Are Higher Today

1. Part of the answer is simple inflation. Things cost many times more today than they did 40 years ago.

2. Another part of the answer is better agents. Back in 1950, all an agent had to do in order to sell real estate was pass a short test, rent an office, and put out a sign. Today, agents' tests often last several days. There may be college or night school requirements,

and there may also be apprenticeship requirements. Even the cost of the license itself has gone up in some areas.

3. Finally, there are additional selling costs today. Today, agents must pay for errors and omission insurance and several kinds of malpractice insurance. Also, they must have an attorney on call, something that almost no one did back in 1950.

Thus if agents ask for a higher commission today than they did 50 years ago, there is some justification for it.

Commission Splitting

Besides, the agent may not get the whole commission.

While you may deal with only one listing agent, by the time your house is sold, there may be as many as four agents involved. (In the vast majority of cases, at least two agents are involved.)

Typically the commissions are split between these agents. The splits vary, with 50-50 being typical, although 60-40 splits (with 60 percent going to the selling agency and 40 percent to the listing agency) are also common. And, for really good agents, 80/20 or even 90/10 between the agent and his or her office is not unusual.

Let's say you sell your home for $200,000. There happen to be two different brokers involved and two different salespeople. (You listed with a salesperson, and the buyer bought through a salesperson.)

Here's how a typical split of a 6 percent commission might work out.

Typical Commission Split

1.5% to the listing salesperson	$ 3,000
1.5% to the listing broker	3,000
1.5% to the selling salesperson	3,000
1.5% to the selling broker	3,000
6% total commission	$12,000

Instead of a whopping $12,000 being paid to one person, four agents each get $3000. If the agent is to make $60,000 a year selling houses, that means that he or she has to make 20 deals just like yours. That's a lot of deals for an agent.

It's important to understand that I'm not trying to justify higher commissions. I'm simply pointing out that in many cases the commissions aren't as high as they appear to be on the surface.

TIP—SOME AGENTS MAKE MORE

Sometimes really good agents will negotiate a better split with their broker. Splits of as high as 80 or 90 percent between the agent and his or her office are not uncommon for top agents.

What about Discount Brokers?

In many areas of the country, discount brokers are available. Often, the rate these brokers charge may be half the normal commission rate. For example, if the typical rate in your area is 6 percent, they may charge only 3 percent. On a $200,000 house, that could mean the difference between a $12,000 commission and a $6000 commission. It could save you plenty. Why not go with a discounter?

You can, and I suggest you do, if you're trying to sell your home by yourself, as described in Chapter 9. A discounter may provide just the limited services that you need. But remember, using a discount broker works best in a hot market. As the market cools off, the discounted listing becomes less and less appealing. The reason is that discounters usually (but not always) also provide fewer services.

Consider this true experience. I was looking for a rental home to buy in a market that I could only describe as warm. I was working with an agent, and he was showing me this house and that. I happened to glance over at his listing book (a book that contains pictures as well as listings of homes for sale), and I noticed that he always seemed to skip over one page that presumably contained homes in the price range I was looking for. After a time, I asked him if I could look at that book. He hesitated, then complied. He explained that he wasn't supposed to show it to someone who wasn't an agent in his area. I suspected that he showed it to anyone who asked.

I immediately turned to the page he had been skipping. In addition to others, it contained two homes that looked ideal for my needs. I asked him why we hadn't looked at them. We could, he explained, only he didn't think they were right for me. When I looked more closely at the listing, I saw that they were both listed by discounters for a reduced commission. The truth was, they weren't right for *him*!

That wasn't right. An agent who is showing buyers property owes a loyalty to them and should show them all the houses that are suitable for them. In theory, the agent should never shy away from a house that might be ideal for the buyers but that provides a lower commission. That's unethical and may even be illegal. The actual practice, however, is sometimes considerably different from the theory.

Can You Handle the Reduced Service?

In addition to reducing the potential exposure to your property, many discount brokers will reduce the services they offer you. For example, they may not be willing to negotiate with the buyers for you. That could be up to you. Or they may ask you to pay for advertising (which, it may turn out, benefits only them). Or they may not be willing to work with buyers to secure financing or to move a deal through escrow.

In short, a discounter may not be able to afford to give you everything a full-service broker offers, because you aren't paying enough. On the other hand, perhaps you don't need full service. Perhaps what you need is partial service, because you're selling your home on your own.

My advice is to let yourself be guided by your needs. If you want a broker to handle your sale, go to a full-service, full-commission broker. On the other hand, if you're willing to handle some of the heavy lifting yourself, then by all means try a discounter.

Full Service at Discount?

On the other hand, some companies such as "Assist-To-Sell" claim to offer virtually full services but at a discounted price. The say they make up on volume what they lose on a lower commission. Some sellers swear by the service they perform. It's something to at least consider.

Reasons for Using a Discounter

- You pay a lower commission.
- You don't need a full-service broker.
- You're willing to do some of the work yourself.

Reasons for Using a Full-Service Agent

- Your house may get more exposure and advertising.
- You don't want to do any of the selling work yourself.
- You're willing to pay the price.

Understanding the Listing Agreement

In addition to agreeing on a commission rate, there's the matter of agreeing to the terms of the listing. These are spelled out in a listing agreement that the agent will want you to sign.

There are a variety of types of listing that an agent can offer you. (No, there isn't just one standard listing that they all use.)

Each type of listing has its own pluses and minuses and should be considered in light of your specific needs. The listing agreement will normally say right on its face what type it is. You can negotiate the type of listing agreement with the agent.

Exclusive Right to Sell

An exclusive-right-to-sell listing is the type that almost all agents prefer. It is also the type that many listing services prefer. It means the following: *If the agent or anyone else (including you) sells the house, you owe the agent a commission.* This includes people to whom you showed the house while the listing was in effect, even if you sell the house after the listing expires and for a period of time afterward.

In other words, with this type of listing, you ensure the agent a commission if the house is sold. The only way the agent does not get a commission is if there is no sale. Sellers tend to dislike this type of listing agreement because they feel it's unfair. Agents, on the other hand, like it because they feel protected. Most agents are willing to put forth 100 percent effort only if they get this type of listing. If I'm confident in the agent, I don't hesitate to give this type of listing as long as it's not for more than 90 days.

Exclusive Agency

With this type of listing, *if the agent sells the house, you owe a commission. If you yourself sell it to someone the agent didn't show it to, you don't owe a commission.* Now, you may be thinking, there's a listing that's more to my liking.

Yes and no. Agents have good reasons for not liking this type of listing. They may bring buyers to your home who tell them that they're not interested in purchasing. Later, the buyers come to you and negotiate a sale. You claim that no commission is due because you had no knowledge that the agent had showed these buyers the home; they dealt directly with you. The agent claims that a commission is due because he or she found the buyer.

In this case, the agent is right. But to get that commission, the agent might have to go to arbitration or even to court. There are certain to be hard feelings along the way, and agents are very concerned about their reputation in a community. They don't like it to be known that they're putting pressure on someone to collect a commission, even if the commission is justified. Thus most agents simply won't work (or won't work hard) on this type of listing.

An exclusive agency listing is sometimes appropriately used when you have a buyer or buyers who you think might be interested in purchasing, but who haven't yet committed. You want to list the property and get it onto the market, but you want to exclude paying a commission for those buyers that you've already found.

Open Listing

With this type of listing, *you agree to pay a commission to any broker who brings you a buyer and to pay no commission if you find the buyer.* Some sellers think this is a good type of listing, because you can give it to any agent.

Most agents, however, won't devote 10 minutes of their time to this kind of listing. If a buyer should show up whom they can't interest in any other piece of property, then they'll bring that buyer to you as a last-chance effort to get a commission. The opportunity to do work and not get paid for it is so great with this type of listing that agents in general just don't want to bother with it.

About the only time this type of listing is used is for bare land, where the chances of selling are very slim and it could take years to produce a buyer.

You might simply let every agent know that the property is for sale and you'll pay a commission, but that you're not willing to give any one of them an "exclusive."

Guaranteed-Sale Listing

A guaranteed-sale listing isn't a separate type of listing. It can be any of the types previously discussed, although it is usually the exclusive right to sell. *The listing simply includes a separate clause saying that if the property isn't sold by the end of the listing term, then the agent agrees to buy it from you for a set price* (usually the listing price), less the commission.

Although widely used at one time, this type of listing is often frowned upon today because of the potential conflict of interest. The reason is simple: While an honest agent can use the guaranteed-sale listing to induce you to list, a dishonest agent can use it to gain a larger-than-expected commission.

A dishonest agent may induce an unwary seller to list, then take no action to sell the property. When the listing expires, the agent buys the house at a previously guaranteed low price and later resells it at a much higher price. This is particularly a problem when the listing calls for the agent to buy the property for less than the listed price (justified by the supposed "fact" that because it didn't sell for the listed price the price was too high).

If your agent suggests this type of listing, insist on the following (which may already be legally required in your state):

1. The agent can buy the property only for the listed price. No less.

2. The agent has to inform you, and you have to agree in writing to the price, if the agent resells the property to someone else within 1 year of your sale to the agent.

3. The agent must buy the property. The agent can't sell it to a third party in escrow, unless you get all the proceeds less the agreed-upon commission.

Net Listing

The net listing is by far the most controversial type. With this type of listing, *you agree up front on a fixed price for the property. Everything over that price goes to the agent.* For example, you agree to sell for $100,000. If the agent brings in a buyer for $105,000, the agent gets $5000 as the commission. But if the agent brings in a buyer for $150,000, the agent gets $50,000 for a commission!

The opportunities to take advantage of a buyer with this type of listing should be obvious. An unscrupulous agent could get a listing for a low price and then sell for a high one, getting an unconscionable commission.

A net listing is sometimes useful for a "hopeless" property. For one reason or another, the property just isn't salable. So the seller tells the agent, "Be creative. Find a buyer. Here's what I want. Everything else is yours." In such an arrangement, you as the seller should insist (if state law doesn't already require it) that you be informed of the final selling price and that you agree to it in writing.

The easiest way to handle a net listing is simply to avoid it.

Which Type of Listing Should I Give?

The type of listing that's best for you depends, of course, on your situation and that of your property. It's a surprise to most sellers that in 95 percent of the cases, the listing that is likely to get you the best results is the exclusive right to sell.

With this type of listing, you do give up your right to sell the property by yourself. But in exchange you get the best chance of having the agent put forth his or her best efforts to complete the sale.

If you give this type of listing, you want to be sure that your agent puts your house on a listing service (such as the Multiple Listing Service or whatever cooperative system is in use in your area). This guarantees that your house will get the widest possible exposure.

TIP—COBROKING— YES!

 In the trade, allowing other agents to work on a listing is called *cobroking* it. Be sure your agent agrees to cobroke your property with all other agents.

TRAP—HOLD BACK
THE LISTING—NO!

An old line that some agents use is to tell you, "To give you a better chance at a quick sale, I'll hold back the listing from the cooperative listing service for a few weeks. This means that all the agents in my office will work harder on it. It's really a better opportunity for you, the seller." Don't believe it. It's just a ploy to give the listing agent a chance to sell your property without having to split the commission. During those few weeks before your house gets on the cooperative system, your agent may indeed be knocking him- or herself out trying to sell it. But that's only one agent. When the property is listed on the service, as many as 1000 or more agents will be aware that your house is for sale. One of them may already have a buyer who is looking for just what you've got.

Don't let the agent hold back (also sometimes called "vest-pocketing") your listing. Insist that it be given the widest possible exposure at the earliest possible time.

Do You Understand the Listing Agreement?

The listing agreement is often several pages long and may contain a considerable amount of legalese. However, there are a number of points that it should contain and that you should watch out for.

What to Look for in a Listing Agreement

1. *Price.* The listing agreement should specify the price that you expect to receive for your property.

2. *Deposit.* The agreement should indicate how large a deposit you expect from a buyer. It should also indicate that the agent may hold the deposit, but that it is your money. Usually such agreements specify that if the buyer doesn't go through with the deal,

you and the agent split the deposit. Try not to insist on a large deposit—it may simply restrict the number of offers you get.

3. *Terms.* It's important that the terms that you are willing to accept are spelled out. For example, if you want only cash, your listing agreement should say that. If you are willing to accept a second mortgage as part of the purchase price, it should specify that as well. In actual practice, this doesn't preclude an agent from bringing you a buyer who offers other terms. It just means that you don't have to accept such a buyer.

4. *Title insurance.* Today almost all property sold has title insurance. The only questions are which title company to use and who is going to pay for it. In most areas, title insurance costs are split between buyer and seller, although in some states the seller pays them. Find out what is commonly done in your area. Just be sure you don't pay for title insurance if you don't need to!

5. *Keybox.* Buyers come by when they're ready, not when you're ready. Therefore, it's a good idea to allow the agent to show the property even when you're not home. Since there may be many cooperative agents, the common way of handling this is to have a keybox installed. The listing agreement asks you to give permission for a keybox. Be aware, however, that you are opening up your home to a great many people. Agents and buyers represent a broad spectrum of people. Just as in the general population, there are those in real estate who are scrupulously honest and a few who are dishonest. While the incidence of theft from homes with keyboxes installed is small, it does occasionally occur. Therefore, during the time you have a keybox on your home, you are well advised to remove all valuables. *Note:* In many listing agreements the agents specifically disclaim responsibility for loss due to improper use of a keybox.

6. *Sign.* You should give permission for the agent to install a reasonable sign in your front yard. It's an excellent method of attracting buyers—perhaps the best.

7. *Arbitration and attorney's fees.* Typically these agreements call for arbitration in case of a dispute, and state that in the case of a lawsuit, the prevailing party will have his or her attorney's costs

paid by the losing party. Read this wording carefully. You may want to ask an attorney if you should sign or change it.

8. *Disclosure.* The listing agreement should also list the various disclosures that you as a seller must make to a buyer in your state. (These are covered in Chapter 6.)

9. *Equal housing disclosure.* You must be in compliance with federal and state antidiscrimination laws when you list your property.

10. *Beginning and expiration date.* Perhaps the most critical part of the document is the clause that states when the listing you are giving expires. It should be a written-out date—"June 1, 2004," not "in 3 months." If the date isn't inserted, the agent could insist that the listing that you intended to be for 3 months is actually for much longer. I suggest never giving a listing for more than 3 months. In most markets that should be enough time for a good agent to find a buyer. If there are extenuating circumstances, at the end of the 3-month period, you might want to extend the listing for an additional 3 months. Or you might want to secure the services of a different agent.

11. *Commission.* The agreement will state the percentage of commission that you've agreed upon. Beware of a clause right next to it that may state something to the effect that if you take your house off the market for any reason, you owe the agent a fee that is then written in. This is a "liquidated damages" clause, and it means that although you may not have to pay the full commission, if you decide not to sell, you are committing yourself to paying something, often a substantial amount of money. Have your attorney check this out.

12. *Transaction fee.* This is a fee that brokers have been tacking on that is paid directly to their office. It's often around $500. It's over and above the commission. I personally feel it is unfair to ask sellers to pay this.

    Brokers charge this fee because they are paying their salespeople higher commissions, leaving less for their overhead. However, that's their problem, not yours. I wouldn't sign any listing with a transaction fee in it.

In addition to the listing agreement itself, most agents will provide you with an agent's disclosure document stating whether the agent is a seller's, buyer's, or dual agent. Recheck Chapter 3 if you're not sure about this.

Listing Danger Signals

1. Long-term listings.

2. Very high commissions.

3. Pressure on you to sign. If the broker pressures you to sign the listing, think what she or he will do when a bad offer comes in.

4. A lister who is willing to accept any sales price on the listing, even though you know it's too high. The lister just wants you to sign and hopes that after a month or so, when you don't sell, you'll drop your price.

5. Hedging on the disclosures, saying that you can trust him or her to look out for your interests.

6. Insisting on a listing (net or guaranteed sale) that allows the broker to make a higher commission without letting you know that he or she needs your written permission.

7. Wanting your power of attorney to sign a deal. If you give up your power of attorney, the agent could accept an offer for you that you really don't want.

8. Transaction fee. Get this thrown out before you sign, or go to a different agency that doesn't charge it.

TIP—KNOW WHEN YOU OWE THE COMMISSION

It's important to be as specific as possible in the sales agreement about when the commission is earned. Typically it's when the agent has produced a buyer who is "ready, willing, and able" to purchase. However, this means that if you refuse to sell, you could still owe a commission. In the recent hot market, many sellers have negotiated a clause that says that the commission is earned only when the sale is concluded and escrow closes.

TRAP—BEWARE OF THE AGENT WHO INSISTS ON A LONG LISTING

An agent who does this could be a "lister," an agent who simply takes listings and lets them sit. Giving a longer listing might mean that it will take longer to sell your house. My feeling is that no really good agent will normally want more than 3 months to sell a house in a stable market. If the house doesn't sell during that period, it could be overpriced or there could be some problem with it that will keep it from selling indefinitely—so that it might not be worth the agent's time to bother with it. Wanting a long-term listing is a danger signal.

5
Winning the Negotiations

You finally have an offer!

You got a call. There's an offer on your home. An agent is going to bring it by in just a short while.

Hooray! You're finally on your way out of this house and on with your life. You can hardly wait. At last it's over. The long ordeal has ended.

Wrong!

If you're like most sellers, the most difficult part of selling your home has just begun. When that agent or buyer comes over and you take a look at that offer, be prepared to be unsatisfied. It's very rare for an offer to have everything you're looking for. Even in a hot market, even if the offer is for full price, you may feel that you need, want, and can get more.

If you're in a cold market, you'd better be sitting down when that offer comes in. It's likely to be for a price much lower than you want to accept with terms that could be onerous to you. In other words, the offer has every chance of being unacceptable.

Only now does the real process of selling your house begin. You have to negotiate with the buyers to get what you want and need.

The Counteroffer

In real estate, negotiations take the form of counteroffers. The way the buyers tell you that they're interested in your property is the offer. The way you tell them that their offer is unacceptable, but that you're willing to negotiate, is the counteroffer.

Counteroffers often fly back and forth between buyer and seller, sometimes stretching into the wee hours of the morning. I've heard many sellers complain that the negotiations were the hardest, the most painful part of the entire sales procedure. One even moaned that it was worse than getting a tooth filled without anesthetic!

Our goal in this chapter is to take the pain out of negotiating and to get the best deal for you.

Of course, you could be lucky. A buyer could simply fall in love with your property and offer full price and just what you want in the way of terms. But, quite frankly, that's not the way it usually works. In the vast majority of deals, it's now time to slug it out.

What Do You Want?

In most negotiations there are winners and there are losers. Often the losers don't even know that they have lost for days or weeks after the negotiation is over. But the winners always know that they have won. The reason is simple: The winners define winning before they start.

In your case, you must know what you want. And in the event that you cannot get it, you must also create a tentative fallback position—the minimum you will accept.

TRAP—ALWAYS BE FLEXIBLE

You never know what the buyers will offer. Consequently, it's a mistake to have a rigid fallback position, saying, "I'll not take a penny less, no matter what!" Maybe the buyers will offer you less than you want, but in a creative scheme that you had never considered and that has all sorts of other possibilities. Be open and consider all offers.

Let's face it: The price you're asking for your home and the terms you're demanding are part realism and part hope. What you must now do is get more realistic. Let's say that houses like yours have been selling in the $160,000 to $165,000 price range. So you put your house up for $165,000. That's hope. Now an offer's coming in.

You've got to understand that, realistically, you might have to accept $160,000.

TIP—KNOW THYSELF

You never know how things are going to go and what you will do until you're in the heat of battle. I've sat with sellers who were staunchly determined not to accept a penny less than their asking price. Then, as soon as a much lower offer was made, they fawned all over the buyer's broker in their eagerness to accept. Be prepared for the unexpected, even in your own reactions.

Assuming that the offer is going to be presented by an agent (sometimes both the buyer's agent and your agent—the seller's agent—are present), you should be aware of the subtle pressures that can be brought to bear on you. Remember that, after all, usually neither agent gets a penny unless you agree to the offer.

In most cases where I've been present when an offer is being made, the buyer's agent begins with a statement something like this: "I'm sure you'll agree with me that this is an excellent offer, probably a better offer than you might expect to get at this time. When you've had a chance to look it over thoroughly, I'm sure you'll realize how generous the buyer has been." You could be asking $200,000 and the buyer could be offering $100,000. You could be asking all cash and the buyer could be demanding that you carry 100 percent financing. Still, when the deal is presented, it always seems to be a "good" offer, the "best" offer, the most "favorable and generous" offer, and so on.

I once knew a very good agent who, when faced with presenting an offer that was far off the mark, would always begin by asking the sellers, "Are you creative people?" Most of us are unwilling to answer that we're not creative. When the sellers replied, "Yes," the agent would continue. "I knew it. I knew you'd be willing to look at this offer with an open mind, because it's a creative offer." The number of different ways in which an offer can be presented is unlimited, but it all usually comes down to the same thing. The agent tries to get you into a good mood, a mood of acceptance, and then hits you with the troubles.

There's a Right Way to Receive an Offer

Most sellers have no idea how to receive an offer (which may be called a sales agreement, a purchase offer, or sometimes a deposit receipt). In most cases, they sit there dumbly while the agent puts a copy of the offer, filled with clauses and tiny writing, in front of them and then proceeds to read through it line by line, often obscuring some of the most salient points.

The correct way to receive an offer is to take charge and direct the proceedings. Once you are in charge, you can quickly find out what the strong and weak points of the offer are and then start making your decisions.

When the agent begins, "This is how I like to proceed," interject the following or a similar comment: "This is my house, and I want to proceed in the following manner." Then list what you want to know in the order of its importance to you. Here's a handy list of information items, prioritized in the order in which you may wish to receive them:

Questions to Ask When Receiving an Offer

1. Deposit: How much and who has it? (Is it a serious offer, as evidenced by a sufficient deposit?)

2. Price: What exactly are the buyers offering?

3. Down payment: Cash, and if not, why not?

4. Terms: New first loan? Any seller financing?

5. Occupancy: How soon do I have to get out?

6. Contingencies: Is there anything that could weaken the deal?

As you go through these questions, be sure you understand the answers that are given to you. When you don't understand something, ask for an explanation. If you still don't understand, don't hesitate to ask to have it explained again and again. Only a fool is afraid to ask a question when his or her money is at stake.

TIP—DON'T ACT IN HASTE

If you hear a price that is substantially lower than what you're asking, the tendency is to throw up your hands and say, "No, never!" That's a mistake. Even if the price is low, the terms may make up for it, or vice versa. You seldom want to turn down an offer cold. Always try to counter.

How Do I Tell a Good Offer from a Bad One?

You probably have a good idea of what you want, and if you're not getting it, you're going to decide that this is a bad offer.

Usually, however, offers aren't either great or terrible. They're somewhere in between, with good points and bad points. All of this means that you're going to have to probe to see whether the offer has some fine points in your favor that were not initially brought out. It's usually not easy to decide whether the offer should be accepted or not.

The buyers may give you some things that you want in exchange for demanding others that you don't want to give up. For example, the buyers may give you your price, but insist on onerous terms such as a long-term mortgage carried back by you at a low interest rate.

You have to decide. Is it worth accepting such terms in order to get your price?

Or the buyers may insist that you be out of the house within 30 days. But, you protest, the kids are in school. You need at least 90 days. The agent makes it quite clear that the buyers have to be in within 30 days because they're moving into the area at that time.

The agent says that the buyers won't compromise. (In fact, everyone will usually compromise a little.) Do you want to sell badly enough to move twice—once to a rental and a second time to your next home?

These are just a few of the trade-offs you may encounter. To help you make a decision, try the following decision-making procedure.

Seller's Decision Maker

	Pros	Points			Cons	Points
1.	_____	____		1.	_____	____
2.	_____	____		2.	_____	____
3.	_____	____		3.	_____	____
4.	_____	____		4.	_____	____
5.	_____	____		5.	_____	____
	Total	____			Total	____

List the pros and cons of the offer on this or a similar form. Of course, the assigning of points to issues is going to be arbitrary, and you may feel that it's silly to do it. If so, then at least consider listing the pros and cons so that you can see what the trade-offs are. The use of points is just an attempt to quantify the issues so that you can see at a glance which are more important and whether the preponderance of the points is for or against.

How Do I Handle Contingency Clauses?

In an offer, a contingency clause (also sometimes called a "subject to" clause) is usually bad if you're a seller. A contingency clause means just what it says—the offer is contingent on some act happening that is described in the clause.

A contingency clause is an additional condition (additional to all the boilerplate that's already part of the document). Sometimes it's simply a clause that's been prewritten by lawyers and checked by the buyers. Other times it's handwritten into the offer, and sometimes it's written on the back of the document and initialed by the buyers. Be very careful of contingency clauses.

TRAP—BE SURE YOU UNDERSTAND THE CONSEQUENCES

Contingency clauses are sometimes misunderstood by sellers because they are written in instead of being part of the prepared form of the offer. Be sure you understand all the implications of a contingency clause before you accept or reject it. If necessary, hold off making a decision on the offer until you've had your lawyer look at it and explain the clause to you.

Some Typical Contingencies

Contingent sale. The buyers will purchase contingent on their selling (translate: as soon as they sell) their present home. This is a very weak offer, because it means that the sale of your house depends on the sale of another house with another set of sellers and buyers.

Financing. The buyers will purchase contingent on their getting new financing—if they're already fully preapproved, there may be little to worry about.

Timing. The purchase is contingent on the buyers' being able to move into the house within a set period of time. This may be good or bad, depending on your own plans.

Disclosures/inspections. The buyers will purchase only if they approve your disclosures and their professional inspection. Typically they will ask for a set period of time for this, usually a couple of weeks. You probably can't sell without this contingency.

Frivolous. The buyers will purchase contingent on Uncle Todd's cow delivering a new calf. Forget it.

Contingency clauses are ways for the buyers (and sometimes the sellers) to get out of the deal. When buyers insist on a contingency clause, it's like telling you, "Yes we'll buy, *if.*" It's the *if* that's the killer.

Your goal is to let as few of the buyers' contingency clauses as possible into the agreement and to limit by time and performance those that are included. Let's look at that more closely.

Limiting the Contingency Clauses

Smart buyers will put few contingency clauses into an agreement; foolish or nervous buyers may put many. The more such clauses you have in an offer that is presented to you, the more you need to be wary.

How do you handle contingency clauses? My suggestion is that you examine each one carefully and ask yourself three questions.

Questions to Ask Yourself about Contingencies

1. Is the contingency reasonable? Making the purchase contingent upon getting financing is reasonable. Making it subject to Uncle Todd's coming down and looking at the house in the next month or two isn't.

2. Does this contingency negate the value of the offer? The buyers offer all cash, contingent upon their final approval of the property 1 day before closing. There's no deal here, since the buyers can refuse the property at their option at almost any time.

3. Can I live with the contingency, or should I limit it? You can limit the contingency by insisting that it be performed within a specified time, say 7 days. Or, you can demand that it be completely removed.

TIP—YOU'RE IN THE DRIVER'S SEAT

Remember, the offer to purchase is just that—an offer. You're not compelled to accept. The offer has no binding effect on you until you sign. (Keep in mind, however, that if the offer is for full price and all the terms you demanded in your listing, you could be obligated to pay a commission even if you don't sign!)

TRAP—YOU CAN'T BOTH ACCEPT AND COUNTER AN OFFER

Once you change the offer in any way, even by doing something so simple as putting a time limit on a contingency, you have effectively declined the offer. What you write in is now a new counteroffer, which must be submitted to the buyers and which *they* are under no obligation to accept.

If for any reason you can't live with the contingency as it now stands (it's not reasonable, or it negates the rest of the offer), then you must take action. Just remember, however, that by taking action, you may be rejecting an offer that may never again be presented. If the buyers don't like what you counter with, they are under no obligation to accept it. They can simply pick up their marbles and leave.

How Do I Make a Counteroffer?

When an offer to purchase is presented to you, you really have only three choices.

Your Choices When You Receive an Offer

1. You can accept it exactly as it is.

2. You can reject it.

3. You can reject it and then counter with an offer of your own.

Remember, *you cannot both accept the offer and make changes in it.* As soon as you make any changes at all to the offer presented by the buyers, it's a brand new offer. You may, for example, like the offer—only the buyers want you out by the twentieth, which is a Friday. You change it to the twenty-first, which is a Saturday, to give yourself more time to move. You've created a counteroffer.

When you reject the buyers' offer, they have every right to simply walk away from the potential deal. They wanted the date to be Friday the twentieth so that *they* would have time to move. They won't budge. Besides, in the interim they've found a house that they like more than they like yours, so they're not interested anymore. You've lost the deal.

TIP—TRY HARD TO ACCEPT

If you can possibly live with it, it's usually a good idea to accept the offer as it is presented. This assumes, of course, that the price, terms, and contingencies are all within your parameters. In other words, if the deal is very close to what you want, you may be making a mistake if you try to get the last penny or the last favorable term. By going for everything you want with a counteroffer, you risk losing what otherwise may be a sure deal.

Don't be confused by the physical form of the counter. A counter is a separate new offer. Only this time, instead of the buyers' making an offer to you, you are making an offer to them.

This can be confusing, since many agents write the counteroffer on the back of the original offer (or on an attached page), adding language to the effect that "seller accepts offer with the following changes." Then the changes are listed. It all sounds like you've accepted something.

In truth, you've rejected the offer and are presenting a new offer to the buyer. However, psychologically, many agents feel that if the new offer comes back on the same document and it appears that there are only a few changes, the buyers may be more willing to accept it. This is probably good psychology, although it makes for messy offers, particularly if the buyers then recounter your offer.

The important thing to remember is that each time you counter and each time the buyers counter, it's a new offer, regardless of how similar to the old offers it may be. You may end up only $100 apart. But if one of you disagrees, there is no deal.

Counter When You Must

There's only one time to counter, and that's when you can't accept the offer that's presented. In my opinion, you should almost never reject an offer flat out without a counter. Simply saying no doesn't give the buyers an opening to come back. Maybe the first lowball offer was tentative on their part. They were just seeing if you were desperate enough to sell at a ridiculously low price. Now they're ready to come back with a higher offer. But if you don't counter, they may feel that you're unwilling to budge at all, that you're unreasonable and impossible to deal with. They may go elsewhere.

**TIP—REJECTING AN
OFFER CAN BE A
STRATEGIC MOVE**

In a very hot market, some savvy sellers do reject offers for less than full price (and sometimes even for full price!). They're assuming that given the market, they should be able to get exactly what they are asking, or more, and that the only way to convince a buyer of this is to give a flat-out rejection. I've seen this work, although you'd better be sure of your market before you try it.

A few years ago I was selling a small home in San Jose, California.

It was a rental property that I owned long distance (usually a bad idea) and that was handled for me by a property management firm. I hadn't really seen it in a few years, although I did stop by just prior to putting it on the market to judge the condition and set a price that I thought was fairly reasonable.

I listed it with a local broker for a price of $215,000.

Almost 2 months later, the broker called to say that he had an offer. When I got together with the agents, a seller's broker and a buyer's broker, I discovered that while the terms were acceptable, the offer was for $187,000, considerably less than I thought the property was worth.

The buyer's agent pointed out that this and that was wrong with the property, that it had been a rental and had been beaten up, and that $187,000 was all that it was worth. My seller's agent sat quietly and never commented. When I asked for his advice, he said, "Better take it. It's the first offer in nearly 2 months."

Both agents advocated my accepting the offer. However, having examined the market and the house, and knowing the comparables, I considered the offer frivolous. While the property might not bring the full $215,000 I was asking, it surely should bring something closer.

I was tempted to simply reject the offer out of hand, since the offering price and my asking price were so far apart that I was almost insulted. However, I concealed my feelings and instead counteroffered. I countered at $214,000, just $1000 less than my asking price.

My reasoning was that the offer might be frivolous, someone trying to lowball me and steal the property for nothing. If that were the case, I would never hear from the buyers again. Alternatively, it might be a serious offer from a buyer who wanted to know how desperate I was to sell.

To my amazement, the buyer recountered at $213,000, up $26,000 from the previous offer and within $2000 of my original asking price! I accepted.

The moral here is that you as a seller never know what buyers are thinking, and unless you give buyers the benefit of the doubt with a counteroffer, you could be passing up an otherwise good deal.

What Should I Counter On?

There are usually four areas in which you may want to make a counteroffer.

Areas to Counter

- Price
- Terms
- Occupancy
- Contingencies

Remember, however, that if you make a counter in even one of these areas, you've rejected the buyers' offer, and they may decide that, on second thought, they want to change some of the other areas or simply walk away.

Countering the Price

Price is usually the number-one concern for both buyers and sellers. Yes, you want and should get your price. Just remember, however, that the buyers feel the same way.

TRAP—"SPLITTING THE DIFFERENCE"

Beware of a little game that sometimes occurs with offers. It's called "splitting the difference." In this game, someone offers you less than you're asking. For example, you're asking $200,000, and the buyers offer you $180,000. Since you had expected to get only $190,000 out of the deal anyhow, you decide to split the difference and counter at $190,000. Now, however, the buyers also decide to split the difference, and they counter at $185,000. What are you going to do? If you split the difference again, you're going to counter at $187,500, which is less than you want. If you reject the offer flat out, you may lose the deal. Splitting the difference has done you in.

It's important that you don't reveal your rock-bottom price too early. If the buyers offer less than you're asking, perhaps you may want to counter at a price lower than what you were originally asking, but still higher than your rock-bottom price so that you can have some maneuvering room.

Countering the Terms

Terms may offer the greatest flexibility. Most often the buyers are seeking a new loan and plan to make a cash down payment. But many times they will ask you to carry part of the financing, perhaps a second or third mortgage for a portion of the down payment.

Just remember that everything is negotiable here. If you're willing to carry back some of the financing, you may agree to their proposed terms, but change the length of the loan or the interest rate. (The shorter the mortgage and the higher the interest rate, generally speaking, the better the deal for you.)

If you carry back "paper" (a second or lesser mortgage), try to see that it includes a monthly payment that is at least equal to the interest owed and that it also includes a *late penalty* for failure to make the payment on time. This will often make the mortgage more salable should you decide at a later date to cash it in.

Counter the Occupancy

Although it seems like a simple thing, I've seen many deals fall apart because of a disagreement over occupancy. You need to stay, the sellers need to get in, and neither will budge—the deal is lost.

If you want to sell your home, you have to be prepared to be flexible in terms of the timing. You have to be willing to give up on your schedule, if that's what it takes to make the deal.

I've seen sellers move out early and live in a motel or rented house in order to make a deal. I've seen sellers stay 6 months longer than they planned (and pay rent to the buyers) because the buyers couldn't get in right away. I've even seen sellers give the buyers a bonus for agreeing to wait a few months extra before moving in.

There is really no reason that an occupancy problem should ruin a deal, as long as you're flexible. Here are some alternatives.

Solutions to Occupancy Problems

- Change your own time plans.
- Move and rent for a while.
- Stay and rent from the buyers.
- Pay the buyers a bonus to change their plans.
- Rent a motel suite for the buyers until you can move out.

Think of it this way: Is it worth a little inconvenience to you to sell your house?

Countering on the Contingencies

In the counteroffer, there are two ways to handle an unwanted contingency clause: the straightforward approach and the diplomatic approach.

You can be straightforward and simply cross out the contingency. You won't accept it. This states your position clearly, but it may offend the buyer and cost you a deal.

TIP—BE VERY WARY OF CONTINGENCIES

A very successful builder friend had an absolute rule regarding contingencies: He refused to sign any agreement with a contingency in it, no matter how innocuous the clause was. He said it was just a way for the buyer to weasel out. It's something to consider.

On the other hand, you can be diplomatic and attempt to limit the contingency. The buyers have inserted a contingency that says that the purchase is subject to a great aunt's coming down and approving the bedroom she'll be living in when the house is purchased.

Fine. You have no problem with that (although it sounds frivolous). You accept the contingency, but add that the great aunt has to give her approval within 3 days.

You haven't insulted the buyers. You haven't suggested that the contingency was a ploy to allow them to get out of the deal. You've gone along with it. You've agreed to take your house off the market for 3 days while the buyers satisfy the great aunt or whomever.

But you've also made it clear that you mean business and that you don't have time for frivolous antics. After 3 days, either they remove the contingency or they lose the house.

TIP—REMEMBER TIME

Time is a great limiter of contingencies.

Or the buyers say that they want a structural engineer to examine your home to be sure that the last earthquake (you live in California) hasn't damaged it. Instead of simply saying no, you won't do that (which will only make the buyers suspicious), you agree—provided that they pay the engineer and that they approve the inspection within a week.

Now you've limited the contingency by action and time.

Limiting the contingencies makes it appear that you're going along with the buyers' wishes, all the while making the offer more acceptable to you.

Specify How a Contingency Is to Be Removed

If you're limiting a contingency by time, be sure that you specify how that contingency is to be removed. For example, the sellers want a soil inspection to check for drainage and flooding. You agree, but you specify that they must provide you with written approval of a completed report within, for example, a week. Otherwise, the deal is off.

Also remember that contingencies work both ways. There may come a time when you want to add a contingency that will benefit you.

For example, the buyers want you to supply a termite clearance, which is pretty standard and usually a necessary part of getting a new loan. But you're afraid that there might be extensive termite damage. You don't mind spending a few hundred bucks to clean up the termites, but you might balk at spending a few thousand. Maybe you'd simply rather not sell in that event. You might write in a contingency that limits your costs in supplying the clearance to, say, $3000. If it's more than that amount, the deal's off. (Be careful that when you signed your listing agreement, you didn't already agree to a termite clearance regardless of the costs.) Cost is another way to limit a contingency.

What If the Buyers Walk?

What do you do when you've been too clever? The buyers made an offer, and you countered at less than your asking price, but higher than your rock-bottom price (hoping to pump a few more bucks out of the deal). You fully expected the buyers either to accept or to counter back. But instead, the buyers have done nothing!

Apparently they are simply rejecting your offer and looking elsewhere. Does that mean that the deal is dead?

Not necessarily. There is nothing to keep you from making a second counteroffer, even though the buyers have rejected the first and have not countered back.

Of course, doing so puts you in a rather silly and weak position. You counter $166,000, for example, and when the buyers flat out refuse, you counter $164,000. It's bound to make the buyers wonder just how low you'll go if they just hang tight. Maybe your next counter will be for $160,000!

**TIP—DESPERATION
COUNTERS ARE
TROUBLE**

When you are making desperation counters, I believe a good rule of thumb is to make only *one.*

Tell the buyers (through the agent, if possible) that you really want to sell and that you hoped that they would counter. However, since they didn't, you're going to make them one last, final offer—your very best deal, so to speak. Make it perfectly clear that this is your fallback position offer. If they don't take it, there won't be any others forthcoming.

Sometimes it works. Of course, it raises this question: What if the buyers now counter at a lower price or terms? (Selling real estate can be so aggravating!)

Ultimately, as always, you have to decide on the minimum for which you'll sell your property. You can't go any lower than you can go.

How Do I Accept?

You haven't accepted an offer until both parties sign the exact same sales agreement. For you, until the pen touches the paper with no changes, and actually for a short time afterward, there is no deal. Until you sign, you can refuse to accept the offer. (However, if the offer is for the price and terms you listed the property for, you could still be liable for a commission to the agent!)

It's important to understand, however, that the deal isn't made exactly when you sign. Rather, it's made when the agent (or you) communicates the fact that you've signed to the buyers. In practice, the agent usually calls the buyers immediately to tell them that you've accepted and then takes them a signed (by you) copy of the sales agreement. Technically speaking, the buyers can withdraw the offer anytime before they learn of your acceptance (just as you can withdraw a counteroffer anytime before you learn of the buyers' acceptance of it).

Sometimes the buyers (or you) are a long distance away. To facilitate the deal, the negotiations may be carried out over the phone. I've agreed to deals from thousands of miles away and then sent a copy of the signed agreement by either express mail or fax machine. Distances shouldn't keep a deal from happening.

Always Keep Copies

The agent (or the buyers) must give you a copy of everything you sign. Be sure that you get that copy and that you hang on to it.

You can't say that you've sold your house until the title is recorded and you've gotten your check, but after the purchase agreement is all signed and delivered, you can kick back and relax a bit. Hopefully, the hardest part is over.

To learn more about negotiating, try my book *Tips and Traps When Negotiating Real Estate* (McGraw-Hill, 1995).

6
Preparing the Seller's Disclosures

If you haven't been exposed to disclosures before, you almost certainly will be when you sell your home today. Most states require, and most buyers demand, that sellers provide a written list disclosing any known (and sometimes unknown!) defects in the home. You'll need to write out that list.

For many sellers, this can be a shock. "You mean I have to report that leak in the roof or that crack in the foundation? Why, it might mean that the buyer will back out of the deal, or offer less!"

Yep, you have to report the roof leak and the foundation crack and a whole lot more. And, indeed, it could require renegotiating the sale, although it will seldom ruin the deal. That's why it's a good idea to present the disclosures to buyers up front, right when they are presenting their offer, so that there aren't any hidden problems that could come up later.

Do I Have to Disclose Everything?

It was not so many years ago that when sellers listed their properties, the first thing they did was cover up all the problems. Holes in the foundation were spackled, cracks in walls were painted over, a few new shingles were placed where water leaked in, a temporary fix was put on a bulging water pipe, and so on. The idea was to sell the buyers on the concept that the house was in great shape. Once the buyers bought it and found out otherwise, it was their problem.

Times have changed enormously. Complaints and lawsuits by buyers against sellers (and their agents) have turned things around 180 degrees. Today, savvy sellers know that if there's a problem with the house that they fail to disclose, and the buyers later find out about it, the sellers not only may have to pay to have the problem corrected (usually in the most expensive way), but in an extreme case may even have to give the buyers back their money and take back the house!

Nobody wants that sort of thing to happen. When you sell your house, you want it to stay sold. And you don't want to be replacing expensive items for the buyers later on. You want a clean deal.

To get a clean deal, you must disclose what's wrong with the property. Some people even argue that you must disclose what you should know is wrong with the property, even if you don't know it!

All of which is to say that today disclosure is a big part of selling. As mentioned earlier, most states today require that sellers give buyers a formal disclosure statement, and some even prescribe the basics of what goes into that statement. (Check with your agent to see what the rules are in your state.)

But even if the state doesn't tell you what you should disclose, you should prepare your own disclosure statement and give it to the buyer—if for no other reason than to protect yourself.

Remember, if you tell the buyer that the house has a cracked foundation and the buyer goes ahead with the purchase anyhow, what's that buyer got to complain about later on?

TIP—LET IT ALL HANG OUT

My own philosophy in selling properties that I own is to disclose everything in great detail, no matter how small the problem appears to be. This has a big advantage in that I never have to worry about buyers coming back at me later on claiming that I didn't tell them about something. It's all out in the open. If there's a problem, it's dealt with at the time of sale.

What's the Worst That Could Happen If I Don't Disclose?

Disclosure is not something to take lightly. I recently had occasion to witness a confrontation among sellers, buyers, and agent that most certainly would not have taken place 20 years ago.

The situation was quite simple on the face of it.

The buyers had purchased a single-family home in what appeared to be a nice neighborhood. They had paid close to the asking price, and the deal went smoothly. At the closing, buyers, sellers, and agent all seemed satisfied. The deed was recorded in favor of the buyers, and the sellers received their cash out and the agent her commission.

About 2 weeks later, the buyers called one of the agents (there were two agents involved in the transaction, both acting as dual agents) and complained that there was a severe problem with the home. The next-door neighbors had a teenage daughter and son. The kids would play their stereo loud during the day and then have parties two or three times a week until early in the morning.

The buyers weren't able to sleep or to enjoy their property. They said that they had talked to the neighbors, to no avail.

The agent chuckled and said that kids would be kids and the buyers should just ignore the noise. If it got really bad, they should call the cops.

A week later the agent got another phone call. The buyers had called the police, who indicated that there wasn't much they could (or were willing to) do and revealed that the former owners (the sellers) had frequently called to complain about the same thing.

The buyers said that they were thinking about demanding a rescission of the deal. This caught the agent's attention. Rescission essentially means going back in time so that all the parties are where they were before the deal was made. In other words, it means taking back the sale of the property.

The agent investigated and talked to the former sellers. The neighbors had indeed been a big problem. That, it turns out, was the real reason they had decided to sell! They had filed numerous police reports against those neighbors.

"But," the agent protested, "why didn't you tell me about that? Why didn't you tell the buyers?"

"Because," came the reply, "who would have bought the house if we'd mentioned it?!"

The agent suspected that she was in big trouble. She went to see the neighbors, who were intransigent. They refused to curb their children.

She went to see the buyers, who had dark hollows under their eyes and who were in the process of contacting an attorney. They couldn't sleep, and if they couldn't sleep they weren't getting the "quiet enjoyment" they were entitled to from their home. The agent had to agree.

The buyers did get an attorney and did pursue the matter, although it never got to court. The rule in their state was clear: It was the sellers' duty to disclose defects in the house to buyers. The sellers should have disclosed that there were problems with the neighbors.

How was the issue resolved? In the end, the agent negotiated with the noisy neighbors to sell their home!

It could have been much worse for the sellers. The buyers might have insisted on rescission, in which case the sellers might have had to pay back all the buyers' money and take back the house! And then there's damages.

And it was all over noisy neighbors, something that wasn't directly a part of the house that was sold.

In recent years sellers have been held liable for a whole raft of potential drawbacks to property that a decade ago would never have caused a raised eyebrow.

Unusual Problems That Should Be Disclosed

- A death or murder in the house that is being sold
- A landfill nearby
- Flooding, grading, or drainage problems
- Zoning violations
- Soil problems
- Bad neighbors
- Anything at all that could affect the value of the property

All of which is to say that if you don't disclose any and all problems with your property, the consequences could be severe.

It's What You *Should* Know

"But," you may be saying to yourself, "those sellers in the example lied. I would never lie. I would simply reveal everything I knew about the house." Unfortunately, it's like getting a traffic ticket. Ignorance of the law is no excuse. It's not always what you know and disclose to the buyers that counts. It's what you should have known and should have disclosed.

Much of the disclosure precedent came from a lawsuit in California (*Easton* v. *Strassburger,* A010566, California First District Court of Appeal, February 1984). The results of this lawsuit were codified in California law and subsequently included in the real estate codes of many other states. The California real estate code deals primarily with the agent's responsibilities. It states, "An agent's duty to prospective purchasers of residential property of one to four units is: to state that he or she has conducted a reasonably competent and diligent visual inspection of the listed property and to disclose all facts revealed that materially affect the value or desirability of the property."

With regard to the sellers, the rules can be even stricter. The sellers often must disclose to the buyers any defects in the property that would materially affect its value or desirability—in many cases whether or not the sellers are aware of those defects!

"But"—I'm sure many readers are frothing—"how can you disclose what you don't know?" The answer is simple: You can either conduct an inspection yourself or hire a competent inspector (discussed in Chapter 7).

TRAP—CHECK FOR
HIDDEN PROBLEMS

Most of the problems with a home that a seller doesn't know anything about involve the various systems— plumbing, heating, electrical, gas, and so on—or the structure. You might have lived in a house for 10 years and have occasionally smelled gas, but be otherwise unaware that there is a problem in the gas system. However, the home might blow up the week after a buyer purchased it. It could be argued that you should have had the gas system checked to protect the buyer.

Do I Have to Fix Problems I Disclose?

While you must disclose problems and defects in your home, you don't necessarily have to fix them, unless they are a safety hazard and liability issues arise, in which case you will almost certainly want to see them fixed.

For example, your lot could have a perennial drainage problem. Every winter, the storms in the nearby hills drop several inches of rain that floods your backyard. The flooding lasts for about a week and then drains away. You could fully disclose the problem to the buyers, and they could decide to purchase the house despite the existing condition.

Or you could be near a landfill that occasionally produces noxious smells. As long as the buyer is made fully aware of the problem and agrees to buy the house despite it, you're probably okay. (What, for example, could you do about correcting the landfill's odors?)

Of course, deciding what must be fixed and what may not need to be fixed could require a person possessing the wisdom of Solomon. However, one thing is clear: The more you disclose to a buyer, the less chance there is for you to have trouble later on.

TRAP— "AS IS" DOESN'T EXEMPT YOU FROM DISCLOSING

Some sellers and their agents have taken to selling homes on an "as is" basis in hopes of getting around the disclosure dilemma. This simply does not work. Asking buyers to take a property "as is" does not negate the need to disclose problems. You *can* ask the buyers to take the house "as is," but only after you've disclosed all the problems and the buyers know what they are getting.

When Should You Disclose?

As I've said, my feeling is the sooner the better. It's important to understand that to avoid any possibility of problems, you should disclose defects or problems with your house as soon as possible. That can mean even *before* the buyer makes an offer. In other words, if you're using an agent, the agent could present your disclosure sheet to the buyer before you accept an offer. If you're handling the house yourself, you could present it to the buyer before you accept any money or sign any sales agreement.

The idea is that the more you get out on the table before the sale, the less you have to worry about afterward. Be sure that the disclosure sheet is made at least in duplicate and that you retain a copy signed *and dated* by the buyers stating that they have seen it and had a chance to read it.

TRAP—WAITING COULD THREATEN THE DEAL

If you hold off showing the disclosure sheet until after the buyer makes an offer and you accept it, the buyer may have the right to take back the offer once the disclosure is given.

Should I Fix the Problem?

The downside of disclosing is that it may cause a buyer to refuse to make an offer or to make a much lower offer.

The solution here is to bring the problem out into the open and deal with it. There are two ways to do this: Either you can fix the problem, or you can give the buyers a cash discount because of it.

The most common such problem that I know of is leaky roofs. You, the seller, disclose that your roof leaks. The buyers don't want to buy a house with a leaky roof.

You can do one of two things. Before you put the house on the market, you can fix the roof. If the roof is basically in good shape, but just has a few leaks, this won't be that expensive. Then you can disclose that the roof used to have leaks, but that now it doesn't because you had it fixed.

Or, if the roof is in terrible shape and must be replaced, you can either offer the buyers a discount or replace the roof yourself. I like the discount idea here because there are many kinds of roofs and the buyers may want a more expensive (or less expensive) roof than you would choose.

TRAP—LENDERS MAY NOT GO ALONG WITH A BUYER DISCOUNT

If you disclose a bad roof and offer the buyers a discount, the lender may require that the roof be replaced before it will fund the purchase. If this is the case, you may have no choice but to go ahead and replace it yourself.

At least consult with the buyers so that you don't put on something that they hate and that will cause them to back out of the deal.

To help sellers with their disclosures, agents and some real estate associations have created their own disclosure sheet forms. (If you're not using an agent, you can usually get a copy from an agent.) These are given to prospective buyers and help the sellers organize their disclosures. Here's what a typical disclosure statement might contain. (*Note:* Check with an agent or attorney first to see if a more specific disclosure statement should be used in your area.)

Mandatory Disclosures

Some disclosures are mandated by the federal or state government. For example, the federal government requires that you give to the buyers a precise statement regarding lead in your property. It lets the buyers know they can conduct their own lead inspection and have 10 days to disapprove the disclosure. As noted earlier, some states also have their own mandatory disclosure requirements. A good real estate agent can help you with these.

Typical Disclosure Statement

Occupancy: Who is occupying the property? If it's a tenant, will there be any difficulties in getting possession?

Appliances and features contained on the property (note that the following is only a partial checklist):

Oven	Trash compactor
Range	Microwave
Dishwasher	Washer/dryer hookups
Sewer	Septic tank
TV antenna	Security system
Well	Wall air conditioners
Sprinklers	Solar heating
Gutters	Fire alarm
Intercom	Gazebo
Spa	Carport
Garage	Garage door opener
Pool	Heater/filter
Window screens	Satellite dish
Exhaust fan	Garbage disposal
Fireplace	220-volt wiring

Roof: Age, type, and condition

Defects or problem areas in the house:

Interior walls	Exterior walls
Ceilings	Floors
Roof	Insulation
Windows	Doors
Foundation	Slab
Driveway	Sidewalk
Fences	Gates

Electrical   Plumbing

Sewer   Heating/cooling

Structure

Other problem areas:

1. Is there a homeowners' association?

2. Are there any common areas? Describe them.

3. Are there any lawsuits that might affect the property?

4. Any deed restrictions or other CC&R restrictions?

5. Any bond obligations (such as a bond to pay for a sewer connection)?

6. Any zoning or setback violations?

7. Any damage to the property from fires?

8. Any damage from flooding or earthquakes?

9. Any settling or soil slippage?

10. Any room additions made without a building permit?

11. Any encroachments from neighboring properties?

12. Any easements?

13. Any landfill on the property?

14. Any common fences or driveways shared with neighbors?

15. Any other problems with the property?

7

Dealing with Home Inspections

Today, most buyers will want—indeed *insist* on—a professional home inspection as a condition of purchase. Should you as a seller oppose this? Should you resist it? Should you attempt to negotiate your way out of it?

The answer is normally no.

Buyers want the home inspection in order to protect themselves by uncovering any hidden problems. But savvy sellers want the inspection even more.

Why? Because it helps sellers protect themselves by showing that they have made a serious effort to discover any problems that might exist in the home. The buyers want an inspection. You tell them to go right ahead. After the sale, if a hidden problem turns up, you can point out that the buyers conducted their own professional inspection, which didn't discover the problem, so how could you disclose it? In short, the buyers' inspection helps cover your behind.

TIP—THE BUYERS
PAY FOR IT

The buyers normally pay for their own professional inspection, which typically costs around $350. So the inspection shouldn't cost you anything.

Thus, when the buyers ask you for a home inspection, don't flinch. Let them do it. If the buyers don't mention it, either get them to sign a statement that they specifically decline to have the home inspected and release you from any hidden defects, or get the inspection on your own and give a copy of the report to the buyers (and get their signatures on it).

Should You Have Your Home Professionally Inspected Prior to Sale?

That depends. If you have the inspection conducted, you'll have to pay for it, and you'll still have to give the buyers a copy of the report.

My feeling is that if you think your house is in great shape and has no hidden problems, then don't bother with your own inspection. Let the buyers do it.

On the other hand, if you think there's a problem with the property or if you have a feeling that some things may be wrong but you're not sure, go ahead and do it yourself. The advantage of doing an inspection before the sale is that you can then select the method (and cost) of the fix. If the buyers conduct an inspection and find something wrong, they may demand that it be fixed at a much greater cost.

TRAP—THE INSPECTION MAY NOT COVER EVERYTHING

Most inspectors are gun-shy these days. They are wary of missing something and having buyers or sellers come back at them later. As a consequence, they sometimes fill their report with so many disclaimers (and sometimes do such a cursory job) that the report is almost useless.

How Do I Get an Inspector?

These days most inspectors advertise in the Yellow Pages and in newspapers. However, be aware that as of this writing, inspectors are not yet licensed in most states. Anyone can be an inspector—you, me, or the woman next door. Therefore, pick your inspector carefully.

Ask for recommendations from agents. Most agents know one or two inspectors whom they rely upon and trust.

Ask the inspector that you're considering for a couple of references. Then call these people. Chances are the inspection was made a few months ago and they've already moved in. Did they find that the inspector missed anything? Were they otherwise satisfied?

I like an inspector who has a general knowledge plus a degree in one or more property-related fields, such as soils engineering. Retired city building and safety department inspectors are often good choices.

Recently, contractors, particularly those who haven't had much luck in building, have taken to house inspections as a way of raising additional money. A contractor can walk through your house, put checks on a form, and pick up several hundred dollars for a few hours' work. Also, if there's a problem, the contractor can then recommend his or her own company for the repair work. It's not surprising that many contractors are doing inspections. (It's usually a good idea *not* to hire an inspection company that also does its own repair work.)

But are contractors qualified? Some are and some aren't. A contractor who builds new houses may not know a great deal about old houses. A plumbing contractor may not know about electrical systems. A cement contractor may know very little about roofs. The value of their inspections may be questionable.

One way of qualifying a potential house inspector is to insist that he or she be a member of ASHI (American Society of Home Inspectors) or NAHI (National Association of Home Inspectors). These are trade organizations that have been endeavoring to raise the standards of house inspectors in general. (See how to contact these organizations in the Resources section at the end of the book.)

What Should I Have the Inspector Check?

There are many areas of the home that sellers should be aware of and that should be inspected either by you or by a competent inspector. These include, but are not limited to, the items in the following list.

Areas That Should Be Inspected

1. Fireplace and fireplace exhaust: Loose bricks, blockage, chimney lining.
2. Electrical system: Circuit breakers, wall receptacles, switches, wiring, light fixtures, adequacy of grounding.

3. Heating/cooling system: Combustion chamber, cleanliness of heater, blockages, compression in air conditioners, motors.

4. Plumbing: Type of pipe and age, rusting, leaks, water disposal condition, water pressure (too high or too low).

5. Sewerage, septic tank, and other waste disposal: Leakage, breakage, blockage.

6. Foundation and structure: Cracks, breaks, leaning, flooding in basement.

7. Additions made without building department approval: Room additions, window or door changes.

8. Exterior and roof: Age and condition of exterior and roof, gutters and downspouts, cracking of stucco, peeling of paint.

9. Doors and windows (including leakage): Weather stripping, hinges, alignment.

10. Drainage and flooding: Slope, groundwater conditions, drainage away from house.

11. Interior: Condition of walls, ceilings, carpets, and drapes.

12. Lot: Safety of fences and gates, any obstructions.

13. Appliances: Age and condition.

Beware of contractors who offer to do a home inspection for a nominal fee, then find something wrong and offer to fix it, usually for a high fee. Some unscrupulous contractors have been using home inspection as a way of procuring business for themselves. As noted, a good rule of thumb is not to have the person who does the inspection do the work. (Also, don't ask the inspector to refer you to someone. That someone could be the inspector's brother-in-law or sister.)

TIP—GO ALONG ON THE INSPECTION

It should go without saying that you should always insist on a written report. However, in truth, accompanying the inspector on the inspection, asking questions, and getting oral answers may prove the most useful of all.

Should I Have a Termite Inspection?

Termite inspections are not really a new part of the home inspection process. Lenders have been requiring termite inspections as a condition for approving a new home loan for decades. A termite inspection and the repair of termite damage have been requirements of home sales for almost as long a time. In almost all states, termite inspectors are licensed, and their written reports must be registered.

Usually the seller pays for the termite inspection and for correction of any damages. The buyer usually pays for any preventive work.

Thus, while there may be little advantage to doing a termite inspection before you catch a buyer (unless you are worried about a particular problem), in a hot market it can't hurt to have it ready to go. Just be wary of paying for a termite inspection, only to find that the house doesn't get sold. The termite inspection is good for only a limited time, typically 90 or so days. If you don't sell within the time period, you'll probably need to get, and pay for, a new inspection.

Should I Pay for a Buyer's Home Warranty Plan?

In addition to an inspection, you can obtain a home warranty that covers the major systems (heating, electrical, plumbing) as well as appliances. A typical home warranty plan usually costs about $300 a year, with the seller paying for the first year. It covers problems that occur after you move out and the buyer moves in.

The cost of such a plan can be money well spent. If minor (and sometimes major) problems crop up, the warranty often covers them, which means you don't have to. Thus, if a water heater goes out after the sale, the buyers don't come running to you for a fix. They contact the warranty company.

Contact an agent for the names of home warranty companies that operate in your area.

8

Taking Charge of the Closing

The one area of selling a home that gets the most complaints from sellers is the "closing." This is the period of time after you've found buyers and signed off on a purchase agreement and before the deed transfers and the sale concludes. Typically it lasts for around 30 days, although it can easily take 45 or 15. It's also called the *escrow period* because it's the period during which your home is in escrow.

During the closing period, a number of things typically happen.

Closing or Escrow Period

- Buyers deposit down payment to escrow.
- Buyers get financing.
- Seller clears title to property.
- All contingencies are removed.
- All inspections and disclosures are approved.
- Deal "closes."

The final step in selling your home is the closing of the deal. This is the time when you sign the deed and a few other documents, the buyers deposit any final monies into escrow, the lender funds the new loan, and the property actually changes hands. (You do not receive your check until after escrow closes.) It's also the time when you can suddenly discover a host of costs that you

didn't anticipate. In this chapter we'll look at the closing and how
to reduce the costs to you.

Can I Control the Closing Costs?

Unfortunately, most of the costs that you will have to pay as part of
the closing of your transaction are going to be arbitrary. There won't
be a great deal that you can do about eliminating them. What you
can watch out for is that you're not paying too much, you're not paying some of what should be the buyers' costs, and you're not paying
for things that weren't done or that shouldn't have been done.
Here's a list of typical sellers' closing costs.

Checklist of Typical Sellers' Closing Costs

	YES	NO
1. Commission	[ ]	[ ]

If you've used a real estate agent and signed a listing, you can expect
to pay a commission. Just check to be sure that the amount is correct. Normally it's based on a percentage of the sales price. It takes
only a moment to calculate it. (Yes, escrow officers do sometimes
make mathematical mistakes!)

	YES	NO
2. Transaction fee	[ ]	[ ]

Of late, some real state agencies have taken to charging a fee in
addition to the commission to cover their costs of handling a transaction. This often occurs when the broker is paying the salesperson
a very large portion of the commission, and hence is trying to recover
his or her costs. However, this should not be your problem. If you
didn't agree to a transaction fee in the listing, you probably don't
have to pay it. In that case, be sure to challenge the charge.

	YES	NO
3. Taxes	[ ]	[ ]

Normally you're required to pay the portion of the taxes related
to the period from the beginning of the tax year until the date of

closing. This is called proration. Prorations are simple to understand, as long as you don't worry over them too much. Some costs, such as taxes and insurance, are ongoing. When a house is sold, you the seller should pay for these costs up until the time the title transfers; then they should be the buyer's responsibility. "Prorating" simply means determining what portion of the costs is the buyer's and what portion is the seller's. A date must be set upon which the prorations are based. Typically this is the close of escrow, although any other date can be used. Since you as a seller often pay taxes and insurance in advance, you can sometimes expect to get money back from prorations. Just be sure that both the proration date and the sum you're being asked to pay or will receive are correct. Beware of any sales agreement that writes in a specific date for prorations instead of saying "close of escrow." If the deal closes early, you could end up paying a portion of the buyers' fair share of costs.

	YES	NO
4. Insurance	[ ]	[ ]

The buyers may be taking over your fire and homeowner's insurance policy. If they are, be sure that they pay you for the unused portion. You often get money back here, too.

	YES	NO
5. Liens and assessments	[ ]	[ ]

You're normally expected to pay off any liens and assessments before title can clear. Make sure you understand any that exist, and make sure that the dollar amounts are correct. If the buyers are assuming any of these, be sure you're not being charged for a payoff.

	YES	NO
6. Title insurance/escrow charges	[ ]	[ ]

You should have been told in advance what portion of the title insurance and escrow charges, if any, you need to pay. Normally this is determined by the custom in your area. For example, the sellers may pay escrow while the buyers pay title insurance, or both parties may split both costs. Be sure you're not being charged an excessive amount or the buyers' share. Also, before agreeing to use a specific title insurance and escrow company, be sure to check out its prices. You might be able to use a less expensive company.

	YES	NO
7. Inspection and other fees	[ ]	[ ]

There are all kinds of inspection and other fees that can be charged to you. These include:

	YES	NO
Termite inspection fee	[ ]	[ ]
Termite removal costs	[ ]	[ ]
Recording deed costs	[ ]	[ ]
Home warranty plan cost	[ ]	[ ]
Tax service contract (if you're giving a second mortgage)	[ ]	[ ]
Attorney's fees (if you used a lawyer)	[ ]	[ ]
Document preparation fees	[ ]	[ ]
Mailing costs (if any)	[ ]	[ ]

There may be other fees and costs as well. The question you need to ask yourself, of course, is: Are these costs necessary and reasonable? The best way to tell is to ask yourself whether the cost is a surprise or not and whether it's big or not.

For example, you should know in advance what the cost for a termite inspection is. You should have agreed to the costs for removing the termites. Similarly, you should have agreed to a home warranty plan, and you should know what it is. And if you've used an attorney, you should have discussed fees with her or him well in advance.

Most of the other costs should be minor. You shouldn't have more than $50 in recording fees. A tax service contract lets you know if the buyers don't pay their taxes and is used when you give them a second or other mortgage. The cost is usually under $25. Assumption fees, mailing costs, and other incidental fees should be very small as well.

TRAP—BE WARY OF "DOCUMENT PREPARATION FEES"

This is a definite no-no. The escrow officer is being paid to prepare the documents. You shouldn't have to pay extra for that (unless you had a special document, such as a lease, prepared).

What Do I Do If Final Instructions (or Costs) Are Wrong?

You've been told that escrow is ready to close and that you need to go to the escrow office and sign the documents. You arrive, and a pile of documents is placed before you. You begin looking over the list of costs, and you see that instead of a 6 percent commission, you're being charged 7 percent. Or you're being charged for all the escrow and title insurance costs instead of splitting them with the buyer, as previously agreed. Or the arithmetic on the prorations doesn't make sense.

What should you do?

Challenge the error or problem and get it corrected before you sign. Once you sign the documents, you have agreed to them, errors and all. That doesn't mean that they can't be straightened out later. But it's more difficult once you've signed.

If there's a problem with the commission rate, it should be a simple matter to solve. Go back to the sales agreement. It should state exactly what the commission is. If there's still a problem, go back to the listing.

TIP—READ EVERYTHING CAREFULLY

I once was witness to a deal in which the sellers signed a listing for a 5 percent commission. However, the agent wrote in 6 percent on the sales agreement. The sellers didn't pay any attention to the commission amount on the sales agreement and didn't discover the problem until escrow was ready to close. When confronted, the agent maintained that the sellers had agreed to the higher rate. The sellers were aghast and refused to sign. Furthermore, they threatened to report the agent to the state licensing agency. The agent relented and took 5 percent. *Note*: This is not a typical story, since the vast majority of agents would never do this and are quite ethical. Nevertheless, it does illustrate the point that reading everything carefully is a must.

Remember, your signature usually protects the other person, not you.

As a general rule, if you feel that the charges are incorrect, go back to the escrow instructions and even to the sales agreement. That is the document on which escrow is based. Ask the escrow officer to correct any errors.

Don't be put off if the escrow officer doesn't want to redo everything, since this must typically be done for both buyer and seller. Yes, it's extra work. On the other hand, it's not the escrow officer's money, it's yours. If there's a mistake in the math, point it out. The escrow officer should correct it on the spot.

Do I Need an Attorney at Closing?

Unless you're savvy enough and experienced enough to handle the closing yourself, you do need an attorney. If there's no problem, then obviously you don't need one. If there is a problem, then you do. Since you don't know in advance whether or not there's going to be a problem, it's best to have an attorney there, or at least on call.

Furthermore, you may need the attorney to tell you that there is a problem, since you may not recognize it yourself. Therefore, it's always best to have an attorney at the closing. It's just a good idea to have an attorney check over any documents before you sign them, and real estate attorneys will often work for you throughout a transaction for a set fee, often around $500 to $1000.

TRAP—DON'T COUNT ON YOUR AGENT TO BE AT THE CLOSING

Don't count on your agent to be there when you sign off at closing. Some agents have learned the hard way that they will automatically get blamed for anything that goes awry at closing if they are there. So they make excuses to stay away. (They're "showing property" or "presenting an offer.") You can't make your agent come to the closing, but you can make your attorney be there.

It's a good idea to ask your escrow officer for an estimate of your closing costs a day or two before escrow is scheduled to close. Since everything is computerized these days, it shouldn't take more than a few minutes to get the costs printed out. It's a lot easier to look them over and analyze them in the comfort of your kitchen over a cup of coffee than under pressure in the escrow office. And you might catch a mistake or two that you'd otherwise miss.

For more information, take a look at the *Home Closing Checklist* (McGraw-Hill, 2003).

9

Selling "By Owner"

Ask any seller what was the biggest expense in selling his or her home and chances are he or she will say, "The real estate agent's commission."

Commissions today typically range from 4 to 7 percent, depending on the area of the country, the service provider, and the difficulty in selling the property. On a home that sells for $200,000, that's between $8000 and $14,000. I don't think there's ever been a seller who hasn't wished that he or she could avoid paying out that much money. And some sellers do avoid it, by selling on their own.

Each year, about 10 percent of homes are sold "by owner," without going through an agent. These sellers either save money on the commission that they would otherwise pay or get a faster sale by lowering their price—or both. You can be among their number.

However, selling FSBO (for sale by owner) takes a certain mindset that not everyone has. It also takes patience and effort. It would be a mistake to think that all you need to do is put a sign in your front yard and wait for buyers to hand you a deposit. To sell FSBO, you're going to have to do much of the work that an agent does. Of course, the results can be quite rewarding.

In this chapter we're going to see what's involved in an FSBO sale and how to get started pulling it off successfully.

Can You Sell "By Owner" in Today's Market?

FSBOs are most easily done in strong markets. If you're in a hot or seller's market, your chances of selling by owner are dramatically increased. After all, if there are more buyers than sellers, it

109

only stands to reason that it's easier to make a sale yourself and save a commission.

However, FSBOs also do well in very weak markets. Here the key is offering a lower price than your competitors (other home sellers). Look at it this way: If your neighbor is selling her home for $200,000 and paying a 6 percent commission, she's actually receiving $188,000 net after the agent's fee.

You, however, since you're selling direct, can offer the buyer a $188,000 price (because there is no agent) and still get the same net as your neighbor. Now, if you were a buyer, which house would you pick first—the one costing $200,000 (your neighbor's) or the one costing $188,000 (yours)? In essence, by giving the buyer the commission that you would otherwise pay to an agent, you get a faster sale.

Can You Really Do It?

If you haven't ever sold a home before (by going through an agent), then I would discourage you from trying to sell on your own. Just as with doing your own taxes, it's better if you have an expert do it at least the first time. That way you can see how a deal is handled and get a feel for the steps involved. This doesn't mean that you can't do it yourself. It just means that the chances of your getting yourself in trouble or ruining what otherwise would be a good deal are too great to warrant the attempt the first time you sell a home.

If you do decide to move forward, keep in mind that you will be on the front line in dealing with buyers. Yes, we're all people, and buyers are just nice people looking for a home. But the moment they become potential buyers for your home, they also become adversaries.

Their goals are exactly the opposite of yours. They are trying to get the price down; you want to keep it up. They want you to throw in the refrigerator, the furniture, maybe even the cat. You want to take everything with you. They want you to finance the house at 3 percent interest. You want them to get their own loan or pay you 20 percent interest.

When dealing with buyers, you're going to have to be prepared to tackle an often aggressive adversary, all the while putting on a smile and keeping a cheerful outlook. The buyers are going to make you sweat, make you worry, even make you fearful. Are you ready to cope with that?

Who Will Handle the Paperwork?

One of the biggest obstacles to selling by owner is the paperwork. In addition to the deposit, there are disclosures, escrow documents, deeds, and a host of other items to deal with. Professionals such as agents and attorneys are trained to deal with these; they handle them on a regular basis and know their ins and outs. You, however, who may sell a home only once a decade, can find the paperwork arcane, difficult, and potentially dangerous from a legal perspective. Is there some way for you to safely deal with it?

The answer is yes. Today you can hire an attorney, or in some cases an agent, on a fee basis (or a reduced commission basis) to do all the paperwork for you. These are increasingly available in many areas of the country.

My suggestion is that unless you are very competent in real estate, don't even attempt to draw up a sales agreement or handle any other documents. The chances of your getting into legal hot water are too great. Plan on spending what it takes (which is usually not that much) to have a professional handle it for you.

TRAP—HIRE A REAL ESTATE SPECIALIST

If you hire an attorney, be sure that he or she is a *real estate* specialist. Most attorneys aren't, and they can muck up a deal by knowing enough generally but not enough specifically about how to handle the transaction.

Do You Have the Time to Sell "By Owner"?

Buyers don't do anything for your convenience. They do everything for their own. They figure that if they're going to spend $200,000, more or less, on a house, then you, the seller, had better cater to them. That means that you have to be ready to show the place at the drop of a hat. A couple drives by, sees your home, and calls. But, you tell them, you haven't dressed, you haven't cleaned the house, and you've got a terrible headache.

Okay, they say, there are other houses to see and plenty of agents who'll show them. *Damn,* you think, and you let them in. Are you prepared for that? (Keep in mind that you have to be prepared to show your property at a moment's notice even if you work through an agent!)

What If Potential Buyers Ask You about Financing?

Today that's easy: Just tell the buyer to contact a good mortgage broker. You can even call several in advance and line them up.

In today's lending market, mortgages are relatively plentiful, and almost everyone can qualify in some way or another. Mortgage brokers are key here. They will talk with buyers, find out about their financial situation, and even provide you with a letter of approval stating how much money they can pay each month and how big a mortgage they can afford.

Ask a real estate agent for a referral to a mortgage broker. (It doesn't have to be your agent—agents will be happy to help in the hope of eventually getting your listing.) Ask friends, relatives, or associates for good mortgage brokers. As a last resort, you can always check the Yellow Pages or go online (where there are hundreds in most areas!).

What about Advertising?

When you sell by yourself, you must do everything in your power to let people know that your home is for sale. That includes giving flyers to neighbors (and making them available in a little box on your sign), putting up notices on bulletin boards, contacting any housing offices of nearby major companies, and even going online and leaving messages on electronic bulletin boards. It also includes paying for newspaper advertising. Here are some tips on that most expensive of venues.

In newspaper advertising (as elsewhere), less is more. The classic mistake that novice sellers make is saying too much in the ad (and paying too much for it as well). I've seen sellers take out full-column, even double-column, ads for their home—unnecessarily spending hundreds of dollars. Perhaps they are hoping to compete with agents' ads.

TRAP—DON'T EXPECT A BIG PAY-OFF FROM ADVERTISING

One of the biggest misunderstandings that all sellers have is the idea that a buyer who sees their ad in the paper is likely to come out and buy their house. Buyers rarely buy homes that they see advertised. Real estate agents put ads in the paper for two reasons, in addition to attracting buyers: to appease sellers and make them believe the agent is working hard, and to get listings! Agents know that callers on ads often have their own property to sell, and they hope to sign those callers up. An FSBO seller, on the other hand, has only one home to sell. You can't sign up a listing, and most of the time the buyers who come over will be disappointed with the home and won't buy. You just have to hope to hit big enough numbers to eventually catch a live one.

Don't get discouraged; play the odds. If you get enough potential buyers through that front door, one of them will make an offer.

Of course, agents are competing with you, trying to lure in buyers and sellers through their own advertising. Since they have many properties and since most buyers gravitate to agents, the odds are in their favor.

Except for one thing: the words *By Owner*.

Buyers love to check out FSBOs (because they smell a bargain and they know that agents aren't likely to show them these properties). Therefore, with "FSBO" (or "By Owner") leading off your ad, you can be well on the way to attracting buyers.

Creating Your "By Owner" Ad

1. Indicate that you're selling FSBO or "By Owner."

2. Give the style of the home and the neighborhood in which it is located (but not the address, for security reasons); include any special features.

3. Give the number of bedrooms and baths in the house.

4. Give the price.

5. Give the general condition of the property.

6. Give one outstanding feature that the property has.

7. Give your phone number or a number where you can be reached. (For security reasons, it's probably wise not to advertise your address.)

Here's a typical ad from a newspaper:

> BY OWNER
> In Maple Schools
> Large 4 bed, 3 bath,
> Newly painted, pool, spa
> Must sell $135,000 555-2134

This newspaper ad is lean and mean. There are few extraneous words. And it cuts right to the chase with "must sell" and the price.

Presumably any buyer who is interested in that price range, location, and schools will find the ad enticing—and will call.

Would a bigger ad be better? Many advertising specialists say that bigger is better because it's easier to see. However, buyers who are interested in homes for sale are usually meticulous in going down a long list of tiny ads looking for bargains, so the cost of a big ad might just be wasted. In addition, a bigger ad might show how inexperienced you really are at selling a home.

Finally, anything else you might add at this point might scare away as many buyers as it attracts. For example, you list that the home has a dog runway. There might be more buyers who don't have dogs and don't want a run than buyers who do.

If you still feel uncomfortable about designing an ad, check out your local library or bookstore. There are at least a dozen good books on designing advertising that gets results. Take out a good one and follow its advice.

Get a Good Sign

A sign is a must. It doesn't have to be elaborate, but it should be large enough to be easily seen by motorists passing by, and it should look good. You can find ready-made FSBO signs at stationery stores for just a few dollars, but I suggest popping for the $50 or so that it costs to have one made up just for you. After all, you're talking about saving a commission worth thousands; surely you can afford a sign worth a few bucks!

When you get the sign, plant it firmly in the lawn where it can most easily be seen by people passing in cars. This isn't necessarily in the center of your front yard. It could be off to the side or even attached to a tree or fence. Don't forget to put your phone number on the sign. Some sellers also add, "BY APPOINTMENT ONLY." That doesn't mean that a potential buyer won't come rapping at your door, but it tends to suggest to most that calling first might be in order. Most of all, don't forget the magic words "By Owner!"

TRAP—WATCH OUT FOR SIGN RESTRICTIONS

Some locales have sign ordinances. These may restrict the number of signs you can use or their size, or you may not even be allowed to put out a sign at all. Check with your local building department or homeowners' association if you have any questions here.

What about Showing the Property?

That's up to you. After all, who else is there?

There are several concerns here, the biggest of which is usually security. You're letting people into your house without really knowing who they are or what their ulterior motives might be. For some sellers, this is no problem. For others, it's a big concern. If it concerns you, get an agent who can screen people before he or she brings them by. And try to have a friend or other family member there in the house with you when you show it. Unfortunately, there's really no perfect solution.

TIP—TRY THE "CALL FIRST" APPROACH

Some FSBO sellers who are concerned about security require potential buyers to call first and won't show the property until they get the full name, phone number, and address of the buyer. Then they call the buyer back. At least that tends to confirm that buyers have given you a legitimate phone number. On the other hand, it can insult some buyers and cause them not to come by.

When you do show the property, welcome the prospective buyers warmly and point out a few of the amenities of the house. After you've talked for a few moments, allow the buyers to wander through the property themselves. (They need to be able to feel that it's their own house.)

TRAP—PUT AWAY ANY VALUABLES

You never know who's honest and who's a thief. Buyers wandering through might just slip a necklace or watch into their pocket and be gone. (You should take the same precautions even if the house is listed with an agent.)

Take Photos

Take photos of your house (one view of the front and another of the inside) and make a list of all its features. Get this copied at a local copy shop, including a map showing exactly where your house is located. Be sure your name, phone number, and your home's "vital statistics" are included. Give a copy to everyone who comes by. A buyer may want to come back later but not be able to find the property, or may want to call you but not have your phone number. This is an excellent method of recalling both.

Have a "Guest Book"

Have a "guest book" located conveniently near the front door. Ask potential buyers to sign their names and give their phone numbers. This gives you a record of who came through so that you can call people back.

If you subsequently list with an agent, you can exclude those people and will not need to pay a commission if they buy through you.

Will I Need to "Open Escrow"?

What could be simpler? After a buyer has signed a sales agreement to purchase your home, just take the document down to a local escrow company. Any escrow company will take it from there.

Don't expect advice, or at least good advice, from every escrow officer, however. Escrow companies are neutral third parties. In most cases, they know their job fairly well. They'll prepare all the necessary documents to close the deal, and they'll tell you what actions, documents, or monies have to be deposited to escrow in order to make the deal. But don't expect your escrow officer to answer such questions as, "Which termite inspection company should I use?" or, "The buyer wants me to repaint the interior, but I don't want to—how do we resolve this?" Those are problems that you'll have to resolve yourself.

Keep in mind that the various people involved in the sale often will provide the necessary information and direction to help with closing. The loan officer, for example, will often help the buyer straighten out credit problems. The real estate attorney will help you clear up title problems. The escrow officer will provide the document for a second mortgage, if you need it. And so forth.

In truth, in most cases, once you have buyers who have signed a purchase agreement, the remainder of the transaction should progress smoothly. You should have few problems, assuming that you know the basics of a sale.

TIP—SET A TIME LIMIT

One compromise that many successful "By Owner" sellers make is to set a time limit for selling by themselves. They give themselves a month or 3 months or whatever. If they don't sell within that time frame, they then bite the bullet and list. This is an excellent plan because it keeps you from wasting time and from losing out on a sale. Maybe you can sell your house yourself; maybe you can't. The time limit helps you answer this question.

Should You Really Do It?

Try this decision sheet to help you make up your mind.

Selling "By Owner" Decision Checklist

1. What's the condition of the housing market in your area?

Hot	[ ]
Warm	[ ]
Cool	[ ]
Cold	[ ]

	YES	NO
2. Are you clear on the steps in selling a home?	[ ]	[ ]
3. Are you up to date on the disclosure requirements, needed documents, and real estate law in your area?	[ ]	[ ]
4. Are you okay with handling people who are looking through your home?	[ ]	[ ]
5. Are you agreeable to letting strangers enter your home?	[ ]	[ ]
6. Will you give up your weekends and evenings to show your home to potential buyers?	[ ]	[ ]
7. Do you have a plan for handling the sales agreement, and who will fill it out?	[ ]	[ ]
8. Do you have a plan for handling disputes with the buyer, both before and after an offer is presented?	[ ]	[ ]
9. Have you worked out the financing so that you can give the buyer options?	[ ]	[ ]
10. Have you contacted an escrow company, a real estate attorney, and an agent, and has each agreed to handle a specific part of the deal?	[ ]	[ ]
11. Have you readied an ad and are you willing to stick a "For Sale by Owner" sign in your front yard?	[ ]	[ ]

For more detailed information on selling FSBO, check into *My FSBO Kit* (McGraw-Hill, 2000).

10

The Lease-Option Alternative

What if you have to move, but the market's so good that you want to hold on to your existing house? What if you can't sell because the market's so bad?

These are just two situations in which you may want or need to hang on to your existing home instead of selling it. You want to have your cake and eat it, too. The question is, how can you accomplish this? The answer is the "lease option."

What Is a Lease Option?

A lease option is a combination of a rental lease on your home and an option to buy, all rolled into one neat package. (There are ready-made lease-option forms available in stationery stores. However, I suggest that if you purchase one, you get an attorney to modify it to meet your specific needs.)

The lease is for a set period of time, usually 1 year or longer, with a set amount of money payable monthly and typical rental conditions. In addition, at the *tenant's* option, he or she can *purchase* the property up to a certain date (typically 2 or 3 years in the future), usually for a price that is agreed upon now. Sometimes cash is put up to pay for the option privilege; however, in a lease option, the lease itself is often considered enough.

Under a lease option, the tenant typically pays a little more than market rent each month, a portion of which is applied toward a future down payment should the tenant exercise the option portion and buy the property.

The lease option has many attractive elements for both the seller of a home and a potential buyer.

Why Would the Buyer Want a Lease Option?

Buyers are typically short on cash. They may not have the funds necessary to make the down payment. With a lease option, however, they can tie up a house, move in, and accumulate at least part of the down payment right along with their rent. (Remember, a portion of the rent typically goes toward the down payment.) Let's take an example.

Lease Option Example

Peter and Sally want to buy your home and are agreeable to paying the $200,000 you're asking. However, they don't have the necessary 5 percent down payment ($10,000). So you offer them a lease option. You'll rent the house to them for $1500 a month (the lease). Of that $1500, $1000 will actually be rent and $500 will go toward a future down payment. When they have accumulated enough money for the down payment (in about 2 years), you will credit them with the money and they will exercise their option and buy the property.

It's a neat scheme, and many times it goes off without a hitch. The tenants pay the rent, accumulate the down payment, and are able to buy the property. It takes the buyers a little longer, but they are living in the property, and, eventually, they end up owning it.

Why Would I Want to Give a Lease Option?

There may be more reasons than you think.

1. You have the chance of a sale in a market in which sales may be hard to find. There are a lot of people out there who can pay a higher rent than there are who can come up with a cash down payment. Find one of those people, agree to a lease option, and look forward to selling your house, albeit a few years down the road.

2. You immediately help the problem of making payments on your current mortgage, taxes, and insurance. By renting out the property, you get immediate income. And because the rental is for more than the rental market rate (the money that is accumulating toward the down payment), you usually have enough to make ends meet. If you've moved out of your home and are worrying about making the mortgage payments, this can be a wonderful solution.

3. You don't have to worry as much about maintaining the property. Remember, your tenants are the future owners. They have a vested interest in keeping the property in great shape. Furthermore, many lease-option agreements provide that the tenants will pay for all minor repairs themselves.

TIP—YOU GET A GREAT TENANT!

You get not only the world's best tenant, but also a tenant who pays for repairs! It's a landlord's dream come true.

4. The tenants may choose not to exercise the option. After several years, for reasons we shall explore in a moment, they may decide not to buy. In that case you, the seller, get the property back, frequently in excellent shape, and you get to keep all the extra money the tenants were paying in rent!

Is it any wonder that many sellers look eagerly at a lease option as a wonderful out in a tight market?

Are There Any Problems with the Lease Option?

Be aware that lease options are not panaceas.

A good rule to follow, in real estate as well as in life, is that if something appears to be too good to be true, it usually is. That's frequently the case with a lease option.

Typically, when you first enter into a lease option, things are wonderful. The tenants pay on time and are quite content.

However, as time goes by, the tenants may begin to see the additional rent as a burden. It may be difficult for them to make the hefty monthly payments.

In addition, unless they have excellent credit, the tenants may come to realize that even if they accumulate enough for a down payment, they may not be able to qualify for a new mortgage, meaning that they won't be able to exercise their option. (Which means that they'll lose all the extra rent money they are paying.)

Once the tenants realize that there is no light at the end of the tunnel, that the purchase of your home isn't realistic, they may bail out. They may simply walk away. In so doing, they could leave your property a mess.

TRAP—IT DOESN'T ALWAYS WORK

My own experience with lease options has not always been satisfactory. I've had tenants whom I had qualified for financing get into financial trouble and leave, almost wrecking the home. Don't think it can't happen to you.

No matter how careful you are, a tenant's bailing on a lease option is always a real possibility. Here is a list of some of the things that can go wrong with a lease option.

Things That Can Go Wrong

1. Tenants can't make the rental payments.

2. Tenants discover, after living in the property, that they don't like it and don't want to buy it.

3. Tenants aren't qualified to get a new mortgage.

4. Mortgage rates rise, and previously qualified tenants now can't get a loan.

5. Tenants stop making payments and move out, leaving the property a mess.

You can do some things that will help to ensure a better ending to your lease option.

How to Protect Yourself in a Lease Option

Qualify Your Tenant/Buyers

Before you go through with a lease option, have your tenant/buyers visit a mortgage broker or bank and get a letter stating that they currently qualify (are preapproved) for a mortgage big enough to make the sale. That doesn't guarantee that they'll qualify later on when they try to exercise the option (rates could change, as could their financial situation), but it at least shows that they have the potential to qualify.

Make the Rent High Enough So That Tenants Can Realistically Accumulate the Down Payment

This is an important point. Say your house is selling for $400,000 and the tenant/buyers need $20,000. If the amount accumulating from the extra rent is only $100 a month and the lease option runs for 3 years, they will have accumulated only $3600 by the time they need to exercise the option—not nearly enough. (And they probably won't have saved the balance on the side by themselves, either.)

Setting the amount of the rent that goes to the future down payment too low is a recipe for failure with a lease option.

Be Receptive to Reasonable Complaints about the Property

While the tenant/buyers can be expected to handle minor problems, major ones need cooperative efforts. The tenants can handle a leaky faucet, but what if a new roof that costs $10,000 is needed? You'll have to work out a compromise and pay part or most of it yourself. If you insist on their paying for unreasonable expenses, they'll walk.

Set a Price Now

It's not necessary to fix a price. You can agree that the price will be what an appraiser (or the average of three real estate agents) says is the value of the house at a future date. But that tends to make would-be tenant/buyers nervous. It should do the same for you if prices in your area have been falling instead of rising.

It's important that both the would-be buyers and you know what the goal is. Maybe it's a price of $150,000 or $300,000 or $75,000. Both you and the tenant/buyers need to know.

TIP—WATCH OUT FOR INFLATION AND MARKET APPRECIATION

It is possible to include an inflation clause or a market appreciation clause in a price. For example, it's $200,000 plus the cost of inflation annually or the increase in housing prices annually, or whatever. Be aware, however, that the prospective tenant/buyers are not likely to look favorably on such a clause.

If I Have the Property Listed, Do I Still Owe a Commission?

Often people who do lease options already have their property listed. How do you get the agent to withdraw the listing?

You could always wait until the listing expires. But usually the agent is more than willing to handle the lease option for you. Indeed, the agent may bring it to you.

Typically the agent receives a fee for the option. It's less than a sales commission, but it is usually quite substantial, perhaps 1 or 2 months' rent. Furthermore, if the buyers later exercise their option, then the agent gets the full commission. (That's why agents like this!)

Should I Try It?

It really depends on your goals and the market. I've known sellers who see a lease option as a way of milking money out of property that they never intended to sell. They purposely get tenant/buyers who could never qualify for a loan and get the extra rent money from them.

Then, when the tenants can't exercise their option and move out, the sellers do it all over again with someone else. I'm not condoning such unscrupulous action; I'm just pointing out that it is done.

For most of us, however, the lease option is another alternative. Just remember that it's not without its problems and it's not a cure-all.

11

The Rental Conversion Alternative

Why sell?

The market's hot. So why not simply keep your home, and go out and buy another?

But, you say, I can't afford to keep two houses.

Why not? If one is rented, it could very well pay for itself. You pay for the other. Suddenly you're a landlord and real estate investor!

Converting your present home to a rental is one of the easiest ways to get started with investing in real estate. And, it saves you the bother of having to sell your home!

How It's Done

My friend Arlie, who owns a house in a suburb of Los Angeles, was recently transferred to Denver. He could have put his LA house up for sale. But the market at the time was strong, and he felt that if he hung on to it for a few more years, there would be a lot of money to be made. So what did Arlie do?

He didn't give up his new job opportunity, and he didn't lose out on the future appreciation on his old house. Instead, he rented out his old house, with the understanding that in a few years, when the market stopped appreciating, he would sell for a big profit. He became a landlord.

This is not to say that becoming a landlord is all peaches and cream. It can be hard work, particularly if you are forced to move some distance away. But it can be manageable. People do it all the time. I've done it many times myself. And it may be your best alternative to selling.

But What If I Need the Money from a Sale to Buy My Next House?

You can get some of your money out, even if you rent your current home. You can get it out by refinancing.

For example, let's say that your house is worth $400,000 and you owe $200,000. Your selling expenses (including commission) might run $30,000, so you stand to net $170,000 if you can sell. You plan to use that $170,000 toward the purchase of your next house.

But instead of selling, you refinance it. As an *owner/occupant*, you are entitled to almost the same terms as a new buyer when you refinance, including taking cash out. (There may be a slightly higher interest rate on cash-out refinancing.) You can almost certainly borrow 80 percent of the current value of the house, and perhaps more. (If you were an investor who owned a rental property, most lenders would loan you only enough to pay off your existing mortgage and closing costs. Being an owner/occupant offers many more opportunities.)

If your home is worth $400,000, you should be able to refinance up to $320,000 (80 percent). After subtracting your existing mortgage of $200,000 and roughly $5000 in financing expenses, you could clear about $115,000. That should help you get into a new house!

TIP—REFINANCE BEFORE YOU MOVE

Whether you will be able to get favorable refinancing depends to a large degree on whether you are an owner/occupant. That means that you must secure all your financing *before* you move from the property. Once you have the mortgage in place on your property and have lived in it for an appropriate amount of time, most lenders don't care whether you continue to occupy it or rent it out.

Learn about Low-Down-Payment Financing

Today, there are all sorts of opportunities for nothing-down and low-down-payment financing, particularly if you're borrowing under a "conforming" loan (one that conforms to the quasi-government Fannie Mae/Freddie Mac underwriting standards). Basically, this means a loan of up to $322,700 today, and probably more tomorrow. Even with a loan up to $500,000 the down payment required can still be quite small.

All of which is to say that you probably don't need to refinance your existing house for nearly as much as you think you do in order to buy your next home. In fact, you may not need to refinance at all! Check with a good mortgage broker to learn your options.

How Much Can I Rent My Home For?

That's very important. Hopefully, you can rent your existing home for as much as, or at least close to, your mortgage payment, taxes, and insurance. This is called a "real estate break-even." It's not a true break-even because it doesn't include maintenance, repairs, and management. But, hopefully, those will be offset by a depreciation loss on your property. (This is discussed further in Chapter 12. However, check with your accountant, as the rules are very tricky here.)

Here's how you determine what you can rent your home for.

Finding What Your Home Will Rent For

1. Contact local agents and ask them. Most of them will be able to tell you off the cuff.
2. Look for rentals in your neighborhood and ask the owners what the rental rate is.
3. Check your local paper under "Houses for Rent—Unfurnished" (unless for some reason you intend leaving your furniture). Look for homes with the same number of bedrooms and baths as yours and in similar areas, and see what others are charging.
4. Check with rental bureaus in your area.

You will probably be surprised. Rental rates are often much lower (or at least somewhat lower) than we anticipate.

Be sure to make your calculations accurately. Here's a little chart that will help you determine how much your basic expenses are.

Rental Income versus PITI*

Rental Income		$_____
LESS: Mortgage(s)	$_____	
Taxes	$_____	
Insurance	$_____	
Less PITI		$_____
Break-even		$_____

*Principal, interest, taxes, and insurance.

If rental income is higher, or if you are at or even just close to break-even, you have a good chance of financially handling the rental of your property.

If expenses are much higher, then you may want to reconsider renting.

TIP—THERE ARE OTHER EXPENSES

Don't fall into the mistaken belief that you won't have any costs beyond PITI. As noted earlier, there will always be maintenance and fix-up expenses. However, hopefully you'll be able to write off the property (see your accountant), and this will more than make up for the other expenses.

TRAP—DON'T RESHARPEN YOUR PENCIL

If it turns out that your PITI expenses are far higher than your rental income, don't decide to "damn the torpedoes, full speed ahead!" When expenses exceed rental income, you move into negative cash flow territory. That means that each month you have to take money out of your own pocket just to pay the mortgage, taxes, and insurance. While this may seem easy to do when you are looking at it theoretically, it's quite different when you're faced with actually spending the money each month. You may quickly come to call that property a "bottomless pit." In the trade they have a name for such houses. They are called "alligators." They just keep biting at you.

Do You Have a Landlord's Temperament?

My friend Philly decided to do just what has been described thus far in this chapter. He decided to convert his existing home to a rental—it made sense financially. However, Philly just wasn't the sort who made a good landlord. He managed to rent the property, but the first week after the tenants moved in, they called him at 11 at night to say that the sink in the master bathroom was dripping and they couldn't sleep. Could he please fix it?

People who rent property on a regular basis would have "sweet-talked" the tenants, expressing concern and suggesting that they turn the water off underneath the sink, then assuring them that a plumber (or the landlord) would be out first thing in the morning.

Philly, however, had just fallen asleep when the phone rang. When he heard the problem, his response was to shout into the phone that they were disturbing his own sleep and that the tenants could damned well fix their own faucet.

At the end of the month, the tenants moved out.

Philly had to rent the place all over again. The next tenants were better: They waited until the second week to call. Their complaint was that the furnace wouldn't go on, and that it was the middle of winter and they were cold.

Philly tried to handle it better this time. He suggested that they build a fire in the fireplace and said that he'd send out a heating repairperson the next day. He did, and it turned out that the heat exchanger on his furnace was broken. He needed a new furnace, to the tune of $2800.

He exploded. He didn't have the cash available. He told the tenants they'd have to wait until the following month, when he would have the money to fix the furnace.

They moved out the next day and sued him in small claims court for the half-month's rent they said they had coming. He tried to argue with the judge, but when the tenants pointed out that he had refused to fix the furnace during winter, he lost.

Philly's problems were not actually financial. They were psychological. (He could have borrowed the money to fix the furnace.)

He never quite understood that owning a rental property is like caring for a delicate flower. It has to be watered and pampered if it is to prosper. Philly didn't want the bother and the headache. He wanted the rental to take care of itself. Unfortunately, that's not the way rentals are.

If you're like Philly, emotionally speaking, then you shouldn't rent out your home regardless of whether it makes financial sense. In the end, you'll lose money, and perhaps even ruin your health, because you'll be doing something for which you are unsuited. On the other hand, millions of Americans rent millions of homes out each year without much hassle or much bother. And they eventually receive significant profits for doing so. It all depends on your mental attitude.

How to Successfully Handle a Rental

Sydney, a young woman living alone, found herself in the predicament of having to move to a new home, yet wanting to have a rental home at the same time. She had heard of the profits to be made from owning real estate, and she wanted to be a part of it.

So, Sydney decided to rent out her present house instead of selling it. She borrowed against it (as described earlier) and used the money as a down payment on another house. Then she was faced with renting out her former home.

Since the house was already in good shape, she didn't have to do any fix-up work. So, she placed an ad in the local paper. It was a short three-line ad that read:

For Rent—Lovely Garden Home
   3 bed, 2 bath with fireplace,
    den, large garage, $850 + deposit.

Sydney included her phone number and soon began receiving calls. She screened the prospective tenants to weed out those who could not afford the house and those who had families that were too large for the property. Then she showed it.

Eventually she got several people who wanted to rent. She picked up some rental application forms from a local real estate agent and had the applicants fill them out. Then she chose the most likely prospect for a tenant and got a credit report on the person.

The credit report was terrible—the applicant never seemed to pay bills. So she picked the next likely candidate and got a second credit report. This prospect had perfect credit, so she contacted the candidate's previous two landlords (the rental application they signed gave her permission to do this) and got good reports. She rented the property to this candidate, collecting the first month's rent plus a sizable cleaning/security deposit.

There have, of course, been maintenance problems. But Sydney either corrected them herself or called in local people to do the job. In over 4 years of renting, she has had the same tenants, and she hasn't had any major problems. The housing market in her area has shown remarkable appreciation. She figures that she has nearly doubled her money by holding the house for the extra time, and now she plans on selling her property for a handsome profit.

All of which is to say that if you're willing to devote a little time and energy to your rental, and use a bit of common sense, it's not that hard to find and keep good tenants and to make a profit on rental property. If you can't (or don't want to) sell your present house when you move, converting to a rental makes excellent sense in many circumstances.

For more details on handling rentals, check into my *The Landlord's Trouble Shooter* (McGraw-Hill, 1999).

12

Legally Avoiding Taxes on Sale

The good news is that real estate offers you the biggest tax break in the world when it comes time to sell. It allows you to exclude (not pay taxes on) up to $500,000 of your capital gain. Where else are you going to find a tax break like that!

> SPECIAL NOTE: The author is not engaged in providing tax advice. The following is simply an overview of tax rules affecting real estate. For tax advice, consult a tax professional.

Under the 1997 Taxpayer Relief Act, individuals can exclude up to $250,000 of the capital gain on a principal residence. For a couple, that adds up to $500,000 providing, of course, certain conditions are met.

TIP—IT MUST BE YOUR RESIDENCE

The exclusion can be taken only on a principal residence. It *cannot* be taken on investment property, unless that investment property was previously a principal residence and meets time rules.

There are some fine-print rules involved in the exclusion that your professional tax adviser can explain to you, but the big rule to keep in mind is that in order to obtain the exclusion, you must have both owned and lived in the property for 2 of the previous 5 years.

That means two things. First, you've got to live in the property (not just own it) for 2 years before you can claim the exclusion. Second, you can claim the exclusion only once every 2 years.

Of course, consult with your accountant to see if you and your property qualify. But if you've lived there for 2 years and owned, chances are you do.

What If I Rent Out My House?

In the previous two chapters we spoke of alternatives to selling: the lease option and the rental. How do taxes affect you in this situation? For the remainder of this chapter, we'll discuss your investment real estate tax options.

If you own investment real estate, you can depreciate it. Depreciating means taking a certain percentage of its "cost" (we'll talk more about this later) each year as a reduction in value. (Of course, there are maximum limits.)

Almost all business assets can be depreciated. Cars, for example, are depreciated over a life span of 5 years. Using the straight-line method, you might take 20 percent of the cost each year as a loss of value.

Residential real estate must be depreciated over 27.5 years. Again using the straight-line method, you would take $\frac{1}{27.5}$ of the cost each year as a loss in value.

Of course, the value of property usually goes up, not down. How can you take a loss on an asset that's increasing in value? A helpful way to understand this is to think of it as a "paper loss." All assets deteriorate over time. Even a house will eventually crumble to dust. So instead of simply waiting until the end of its useful life span (arbitrarily decided by the government), you take a portion of the loss in value each year.

TIP—A HOME'S LIFE SPAN IS SET BY THE GOVERNMENT

The time span of 27.5 years is specified by the government and is quite arbitrary. In the past much shorter time spans have been allowed.

But, you may reasonably say, while the house will eventually deteriorate, the land never will. How can you depreciate land costs?

The answer is, you can't. You can depreciate only the building, not the land. The only exception would be if the land itself had an asset that was depletable, such as gas and oil, and that's not the case here.

Is Depreciation an Expense?

Yes, it is. When you own rental property, you have depreciation expense in much the same way as you have other expenses. For example, here's a list of some expenses that you might expect to incur.

Typical Rental Property Expenses

- Mortgage interest
- Taxes
- Insurance
- Water service
- Garbage service
- Maintenance and repair
- Fix-up
- Advertising
- Pool and gardener service
- Depreciation

TIP—SAVE ALL YOUR RECEIPTS

When you own a house, the only deductions are typically property taxes and mortgage interest. However, with a rental property, almost everything is deductible. You may even be able to deduct a phone, an auto, even business cards! Check with your accountant.

When you add up all of these expenses, you have the total expenses for your property over a month. Add all the monthly expenses together, and that's how much it costs you over a year.

Now subtract your total annual expenses from your total annual income, and that's your profit or loss.

Does Depreciation Contribute to Loss?

It certainly does. As soon as you begin to look at properties out there in the real world, you'll come to realize that finding one where the income even comes close to paying for the actual cash expenses is rare. When you add the paper loss of depreciation to your cash expenses, you almost always find that there's a loss.

Typical Income/Expense on a Rental House

Total Annual Income	$14,440	($1,200 monthly)
Total Annual Cash Expenses	−14,000	
Positive Cash Flow	440	
Annual Depreciation	−7,500	
Annual Loss	−7,060	

Once depreciation is added in, you can be assured that the property will almost always show a loss, at least on paper. In our example, a good property that actually shows a positive cash flow (more money coming in than cash expenses going out) turns into a big loser as soon as depreciation is added.

TIP—IT'S A LOSS ONLY ON PAPER

Remember that the loss from depreciation is not an out-of-pocket expense. It's simply an accounting loss— it shows up only on paper.

In the dim distant past, depreciation was a tax dodge that was used by the wealthy to reduce their sizable incomes. They would take that loss from real estate (which occurred only on paper) and deduct it from their ordinary income. That reduced their ordinary income and, of course, reduced the amount of taxes they would owe on that income.

That tax shelter was eliminated for the wealthy by the Tax Reform Act of 1986. Now it is available only if your income is less than $150,000. We'll have more to say about this shortly.

Depreciation Reduces the Tax Basis of the Property

Let's go back to where we were earlier when we said that depreciation reduced the "cost" of the building by a certain amount each year. While cost is the most common method of establishing a tax basis, it's not the only consideration.

For tax purposes, there is a "basis" for each asset. That is the amount used in making tax calculations for such things as depreciation and, when you sell, capital gains.

The basis for most assets, as we said, is their cost. However, with homes, that basis can vary. For example, there are substantial transaction fees when you buy a home. Most of these are added to the basis.

Or, you may build an addition to the home. This is also added to the basis.

On the other hand, depreciation reduces the basis of the property. Here's how it works.

Changes in Basis

Original basis (cost)	$200,000
Add a room	+ 30,000
Adjusted basis	230,000
Depreciation ($7000 annually for 10 years)	− 70,000
New adjusted basis	160,000

Notice that although the property began with a basis of $200,000, which was its cost, that basis went up when a room was added and, more importantly here, went down when depreciation was calculated.

What's the Importance of the Tax Basis?

The reason that we've spent some time discussing basis is that when you sell, it (and the sales price) determines your capital gain on the property and the tax you'll have to pay.

Your capital gain on the property is the difference between the adjusted tax basis and the sales price.

Calculating Capital Gain

Sales price (adjusted for costs of sale such as commission)	$300,000
Adjusted tax basis	160,000
Capital gain (on which tax is due)	140,000

Thus, to summarize our example, you buy the property for $200,000; add a room for $30,000, which raises your basis; and then depreciate the property by $70,000, which lowers the basis. When you sell, both the raising and the lowering of the tax basis affects how big a capital gain you have.

TIP—MORE CAPITAL GAINS

It's important to keep one's eye on the doughnut and not the hole. What's important here is to see that depreciation lowers the basis, which means that upon sale, there will be more capital gains (and resulting taxes).

All of which is to say that while depreciating real estate can produce a tax write-off, as noted earlier, when you sell, that tax loss comes back to haunt you as a capital gain.

Thus, in decades past, when anyone, regardless of income, could write off losses on real estate, what they were actually doing was converting their ordinary income to capital gains. Instead of paying ordinary income taxes at a high rate, they converted that income into a capital gain and paid capital gains taxes on it at a lower rate.

In case this discussion went by rather fast, let's take it again a bit more slowly. Let's consider just one year. In that year, the property sustained a loss of $7000 (primarily from depreciation). That $7000 was then deducted from the investor's ordinary income. That meant that the investor avoided paying ordinary income taxes (at a high tax rate) on $7000.

Now suppose that the property is sold the very next year, and it shows a $7000 capital gain attributable to the depreciation taken. The investor now has to pay tax on this amount. However, because it was a "capital gain," as opposed to "ordinary income," the tax rate is lower. Thus the great tax shelter benefit of real estate was that it converted ordinary income into capital gains and thus reduced the tax rate.

Doesn't That Work Now?

Not like it used to. First, the Tax Reform Act of 1986 prohibited high-income investors from taking a deduction for their real estate losses. Then the Taxpayer Relief Act of 1997 reduced the capital gains rate (and added a few more wrinkles, as we'll shortly see).

To begin, however, let's consider the rules with regard to taking a loss on real estate as a deduction against your ordinary income.

Active income. The tax law now discriminates between the types of income that we receive. Income from wages or received as compensation for services is called active income. It includes commissions, consulting fees, salary, and anything similar. It's important for those involved in real estate to note that profits and losses from businesses in which you "materially participate" (not including limited partnerships) are included. However, real estate activities are specifically excluded.

*Passive income.*This is a bit trickier to define, but in general it means the profit or loss that we receive from a business activity in which we do not materially participate. This includes not only limited partnerships but also income from any real estate that is rented out. It's important to note that income from real estate is specifically defined as passive.

Portfolio income. This is income from dividends, interest, royalties, and anything similar. We need not worry much about this here except to note that it does not include real estate income.

Under the old law, income was income and loss was loss. Thus, you could deduct any loss on real estate from your other income. Under the current law, your personal income is considered "active" and your real estate loss is considered "passive." Since you can't deduct a passive loss from active income, you can't, in general, write off any real estate losses.

What about the Little Guy?

We've already said that this change was primarily aimed at eliminating a big tax shelter for the wealthy. But there is an advantage that is retained here for the small investor.

There is an important exception to the previous rule. This exception provides a $25,000 allowance for write-offs for those with lower ordinary income. In other words, you can write off up to $25,000 in losses from real estate against your active income, provided you meet an income ceiling (plus certain other qualifications).

Your Gross Adjusted Income Must Not Exceed $150,000

If your income is below $100,000, then you qualify for the entire $25,000 exception. If it is between $100,000 and $150,000, you lose fifty cents of the allowance for every dollar by which your income exceeds $100,000.

Since most small investors have incomes under $150,000, the allowance applies to them. They can deduct their losses on real estate up to the $25,000 limitation.

What's the Other Qualification?

You'll recall that we said that there was another qualification. This is that you must actively participate in the business of renting the property.

This can be tricky. After all, what does "actively participate" really mean?

If you own the property and are the only person directly involved in handling the rental—you advertise it, rent it, handle maintenance and clean-up, collect the rent, and so on—then obviously you materially participate.

However, there are gray areas. Generally, if you don't personally determine the rental terms, approve new tenants, sign for repairs, approve capital improvements, and the like, then you may not qualify.

The question that always comes up is, "What if I hire a management firm to handle the property for me?"

This is an even grayer area. In general, using a management firm is probably okay as long as you continue to materially participate (determine rental terms, approve new tenants, sign for repairs or capital improvements, and the like). If you are going to use a management firm, be sure that you have your attorney check over the agreement you sign with the firm to see that it does not characterize you as not materially participating and thus prevent you from deducting any loss.

Are There Any Other Kinks in the Rules?

On the surface, the allowance and the qualifications may seem straightforward. But, they can be tricky. For example, here are some other considerations:

1. The income used to determine whether you qualify is your adjusted gross income. This means your income after you have taken some deductions, such as some retirement plan contributions (not IRAs), alimony, and moving expenses.

2. The allowance does not apply to farms. If you materially participate in the running of a farm, other rules apply—see your accountant or tax attorney.

3. Those who don't qualify to take the deduction against their active income also cannot take the deduction against their portfolio income. (Remember, portfolio income came from interest, dividends, royalties, and so on.)

So, When I Sell, Chances Are I Will Owe Some Capital Gains?

Maybe, assuming that you don't sell for a loss. However, as noted, the capital gains tax rate has been reduced. At the present time, it's 15 percent. Hence, even if you do have to pay, it won't be a confiscatory amount.

TRAP—TAX QUIRK

There's another quirk in the tax laws. You owe tax on a capital gain regardless of whether the property you are selling is investment property or a personal residence. However, if you sell at a capital loss, you can take that loss on investment property, but you can't take a deduction for that loss if it's on a personal residence!

Is There Any Legal Way to Avoid Paying Taxes on My Profits?

That, of course, is the national pastime that most Americans engage in—finding legal ways to avoid paying high taxes. And, in the case of investment real estate, there are a few loopholes that can benefit the investor.

The first method that might be used is to convert the property from an investment to a personal residence. You can remove the tenants, move in yourself, and declare the property to be your principal residence. After a period of time, you may then be able to sell the home and reap the benefits of the principal residence capital gains exclusion of up to $250,000. We've already discussed this at the beginning of this chapter.

TIP—YOU OWE TAXES ONLY WHEN YOU SELL

Keep in mind that in real estate, you owe taxes on your profit (capital gain) only when you sell. No matter how high the value of your property goes, you don't pay capital gains tax on it as long as you continue to own it. (You would, of course, owe income taxes if you showed excess income over expenses on an annual basis.)

There are certain problems with this scenario, however. The first is, how long must you reside in the property in order to make it your personal residence? I don't know of any hard and fast rule. Some accountants say 2 years, others say longer. Check with your professional tax adviser.

The second has to do with all that depreciation you took while you owned the property. Some might have to be recaptured at a special rate (although the tax code is changing on this—see your accountant). Thus, even though you may avoid paying taxes on most of your capital gain by using the personal property exclusion, you may still owe some taxes on the recaptured depreciation losses that you took earlier.

TIP—TRY AN EXCHANGE

Yet another problem is that very often the investor is not really interested in moving into the rental property. In that case, a tax-deferred exchange, as described in the next section, might be better.

Is There Another Way of Legally Avoiding Paying Taxes on My Capital Gain?

There may be. You can trade your property for another and defer the capital gain from the old property to the new. This is technically called a Section 1031(a)(3) Tax Deferred Exchange.

A great many investors see this as a way of multiplying their profits without paying taxes along the way. They hopscotch from property to property, increasing the value of their real estate holdings unencumbered by the need to pay taxes on each transaction.

TIP—IT'S LIKE GETTING COMPOUND INTEREST ON YOUR EQUITY

Normally, in the sale of one property and the purchase of another, you would pay taxes on your capital gain. That would leave you with less equity to invest in the next property. However, by deferring that tax bill into the future, you can put more of your equity into the next property, meaning that you can buy a bigger and better investment house!

The rules for tax-free exchanges were greatly simplified more than a decade ago by several tax cases, the most famous of which is called the Starker rule. Under Starker, you just go ahead and sell your investment property as you would otherwise. However, you have 45 days after the sale to designate a new property in which you will invest your money. And you have 120 days to close the deal on that new property.

In making such an exchange, there are other strict conditions that usually must be met. One is that you may not take cash ("boot") out as part of the sale. If you want cash out, you must usually either refinance the old property before the exchange or refinance the new property after it. Again, check with your accountant for details.

Another condition is that only properties of like kind can be exchanged—that means property held for investment with other property held for investment. Exchanging an income-producing apartment building for a home in which you plan to live probably would not be allowed by the IRS.

Can I Combine an Exchange and a Personal Property Exclusion?

As we noted earlier, one of the problems with converting an investment property into a personal property is that you may not want to reside in a property that you own as an investment. If that's the case, then the answer could be simple: Just do a tax-deferred exchange of the investment property into a property in which you would like to live. Then convert the desirable home from investment to principal residence.

However, keep in mind the "like kind" rule. A personal residence is not the same thing as an investment house. Therefore, in order not to invalidate the tax-deferred status of the exchange, you might have to rent out the new property for a time before moving in yourself. How long should you wait before converting the investment property to a principal residence? Some tax advisers have suggested 6 months, others as long as 2 years. Again, check with your own professional tax adviser.

Keep Good Records

From our discussion here, one other thing should be apparent: You need good record keeping. It's very important that you keep every receipt and note every expense and piece of income in a ledger.

You may have to prove to the IRS that the expenses that you had on your investment property were real. For example, when you had a vacancy 3 years earlier, you spent $115 on advertising to get a new tenant.

Prove it, says the IRS. So, you reach into your bag of receipts and pull out an invoice from the local newspaper for $115 for advertising. Attached to it is a copy of the ad itself and your check in payment. It's hard to dispute that.

Also, keep all records if you make improvements to the property. Remember, improvements *raise* the tax basis, and this will later reduce the amount of capital gains you will need to pay. (The higher the tax basis, the less the capital gain.)

If you make a capital improvement, such as putting on a new roof or adding a patio, keep all of the receipts. At the end of the year, your accountant will be able to use them to adjust your tax basis upward.

TIP—IMPROVEMENT
VERSUS REPAIR

Just because you spend money improving your rental doesn't mean that you've made a capital improvement for tax purposes. Replacing a water heater, for example, is probably not a capital improvement, it's a repair. Adding a tile roof where there was previously a less expensive tar roof would be a capital improvement (at least in the amount of the difference in price between the tar roof and the tile).

What If I Refinance?

As strange as it may seem, refinancing your property and taking cash out without a sale normally has no immediate tax consequences. You don't report new mortgages to the IRS. You might, however, have less equity to rely upon later on when you do sell and must pay capital gains taxes.

13
Selling in a Bad Market

In any market, a seller can get "upside down." That simply means that you owe more on your home than it's worth. If you sell it at market, not only will you not receive any money out of the sale, but you might have to put money into the deal out of your own pocket just to make the sale!

Being upside-down happens more often in down markets, where prices have dropped. However, even in strong markets, sellers can get too much financing on the property (sometimes up to 125 percent of its value), so that they have little, no, or negative equity. When the costs of selling (commission, title insurance, escrow fees, and so on) are thrown in, they discover that they're upside-down.

If you're upside down and you find that you must sell right away (perhaps because of job loss, transfer, illness, or some other similar reason), take heart. You should get some immediately useful answers in this chapter.

There are six things that you should do immediately when you find that you're upside down.

1. Talk to Your Lender

It's like meeting two bullies in an alleyway who look like they want to fight. You can "put up your dukes," or you can see if you can talk your way out of it.

Talking is a good idea.

If you're behind in your payments, or if you need your lender to make a concession on your loan (accept a short payoff, or less than the amount owed), talking to your lender transforms you from an impersonal name on a sheet of paper into a person. You've got a personality; you've got warmth, humor, and value. In short, even for a lender, it's a lot harder to beat up on someone you know than on a complete stranger.

As soon as you realize that you're upside down and you need to sell, contact your lender. Find out its policy. Find out if it can help you restructure your loan (many lenders will work hard to do this).

Contacting your lender, however, can be more difficult than it seems at first. After all, most lenders are giant institutions. How do you find the one person among hundreds, perhaps thousands, of employees who will respond to your needs?

Turn it around. If you don't contact your lender and you stop making your mortgage payments, your lender will contact you.

And the person making that contact may not be nearly as pleasant as the person you'll find if you go looking yourself.

If your lender is a local institution, such as a bank, the best place to start is often a local branch office. If you know the employees there, they often can direct you to the right person.

If your lender doesn't have a local office, then start calling and work your way through the system. You may have to go through several at least partial explanations before you get through to someone who will listen, understand, and, if not commiserate, at least take notes for future reference.

What Do I Say?

In essence, what you tell your lender is that your home is not worth the mortgage amount, and that you're having trouble making payments and/or that you must sell.

TIP—LENDERS DON'T LISTEN TO GOOD BORROWERS

If you're up-to-date on your payments, most lenders don't want to talk to you. You're not a problem yet. Until you're at least several months behind on your payments, many lenders won't seriously deal with you.

If you're several months behind, most lenders with whom you talk today will try to help you in several ways. They may be willing to allow you to miss payments for a period of time, if it appears that you will be able to start making them again later on. (You're temporarily sick, for example.) Or they may restructure your loan, giving you lower payments. Or they might forgo interest for a period of time. After the real estate recession of the early 1990s, most lenders became quite adept at helping out troubled borrowers.

**TRAP—SOME
LENDERS PLAY
HARDBALL**

Not all lenders are willing or able to help. You may just end up with a hardball lender who says simply, "Pay as agreed, or we'll foreclose." If that's the case, then you need to play hardball in return and say, "If you foreclose, you'll lose money. Let's work together on a better solution."

2. Consider a "Deed in Lieu of Foreclosure"

Another possible solution is to deed the property directly to the lender. The lender can then attempt to resell it. You won't get anything out of this deal, but it helps to protect your credit and gives you an honorable way out. Besides, when you're upside down you have no equity anyhow.

Why would a lender accept this option? Most won't, unless you make it more attractive to them. One person I know, after not making payments for 3 months and being threatened with foreclosure, called his lender and explained it this way: "If you accept a deed to the property in lieu of foreclosing, I'll be out next week and you'll get the house back in good shape, ready to resell.

"If, however, you refuse, then I'll sit in the house, without making payments, for the 5 months it takes to foreclose in this state. During that time, anything can happen—the hardwood floors might get ruined; vandals might put holes in the walls; windows, sinks, and toilets could get broken. Neighborhood gangs might even come in and tear up and graffiti the place. You'll get it back after foreclosure, okay, but you may not like it!" The lender immediately agreed to accept a deed in lieu of foreclosure.

The seller played hardball.

TRAP—LENDERS
HAVE HEARD IT ALL

Lenders are aware of this ploy, and they may go to court to get a restraining order prohibiting you from damaging the property. The order, however, can be hard to enforce, particularly if you abandon the property and damage occurs from vandalism after you leave and before the lender gets possession. However, as part of your loan agreement, you're responsible for keeping up the property.

3. Negotiate a "Short Sale"

A short sale is a different tack. You suggest to the lender that the best way for both of you to get out of this predicament is for you to remain in the property, keeping it in good shape and finding a buyer. However, the house is worth less than the mortgage and costs of sale. Therefore, in order for you to make the sales effort, the lender will have to agree to take less—a short sale.

Will lenders agree?

Probably not—at least, not formally. What many savvy lenders will say is something such as, "Keep trying to find a buyer who will pay off the entire mortgage. But if you can't, and you do find a buyer in a short sale, we'll talk." That's about as much of a commitment to a short sale as you're likely to get from a lender. But it's a good start. Armed with nothing more than this, I would begin trying to sell the house at market, even if it's less than you owe.

If you are successful and you do find a buyer who is ready, willing, and able to purchase on a short sale, write up the deal (or have your agent write it), get a deposit, and present it to the lender. From the lender's perspective, it's really tough to turn such a deal down, provided the amount short is not too great. After all, you're offering a way out that's neat and clean. If the lender refuses, there's the dirty way, which involves foreclosure and the costs of fixing up a property that the lender could get in damaged condition.

**TIP—WORK FROM A
POSITION OF POWER
AND LEVERAGE**

Don't try to get the lender to commit formally to a short sale for a specific amount of money until you actually have a buyer in hand. Then you've got something to bargain with.

4. Convert to a Rental

Here's an idea that sometimes works. Instead of selling at a loss or losing the home to foreclosure, why not try renting it out until times get better? After all, it's certain that at some time in the future, your property is going to be worth more than it is today. Why not hang on to it until it appreciates?

Most sellers have three good reasons for not wanting to rent out the property. First, they want to be done with it, one way or another. It's an emotional anchor to be continually worrying about what's going to happen to the house. Better, many sellers say, to have done with it, even if that means foreclosure. (Bad answer. See item 6.)

Second, many sellers have never been landlords. They may feel that they're jumping from the frying pan into the fire. What if the tenants don't pay? What if they move out? What if they mess up the place? Worst of all, what if they don't pay, don't move, and mess up the place?

Of course it could happen. But I've been renting properties of all kinds for more than 30 years, and, quite frankly, if you take pains to screen tenants carefully, it seldom happens.

Third, in most markets you can't rent a home for enough money to pay for the PITI. (That's mortgage principal, interest, taxes, and insurance.) In other words, it will cost you money out of pocket each month to keep the place and rent it.

True, but it's probably worth it to protect your credit. (Again, see item 6.) And you may be able to significantly increase the amount of rent that you receive by doing a lease option, as discussed in Chapter 10.

Renting your house out may not seem like a good option, particularly when you may have to rent it for a year or more before you're able to sell it. But it might be a terrific solution, compared with the alternatives.

5. Bite the Bullet and Change Your Plans

This is the least attractive alternative for most upside-down sellers. It means that you let your property dictate your future, instead of the other way around.

Some sellers, realizing that they can't easily sell or get out from under, have refused job transfers, have taken lower-paying jobs, or have borrowed money (from the bank or from relatives) so that they could stay where they were, in their home. They don't sell, and they continue to make their payments.

This may mean using up some of your retirement money or the kids' college funds. It could mean a lower lifestyle for a while. It could mean remaining in an area after all your friends have moved away. But it could also mean avoiding foreclosure and the trauma of a forced move.

TRAP—ALL THINGS COME TO HE OR SHE WHO WAITS . . . SOMETIMES

Sometimes sellers just don't want to lose their "equity." They figure that if they stay long enough, they'll get out what they have put into the house. However, it's usually possible to buy elsewhere, in a better market, and double or triple your equity in the time it takes to recoup it from an upside-down property. Quite frankly, I don't recommend staying on unless there's a compelling reason to preserve your ownership of the property. Personally, I prefer moving on with my life, even if it means using one of the more dramatic solutions previously noted. I wouldn't like the trapped feeling of knowing that I couldn't move, that I was just afloat where I was. It's better to take a hit now and get on with things.

6. Protect Your Credit

Faced with difficult choices, a great many people who are upside down with their homes choose to "walk." This is an unexpected application of the motto "When the going gets tough, the tough get going!" It's so much easier just to let the bank take the house back.

Yes, it is—until you want to buy another house. Then you may find that you've thrown out the baby with the bath water. The truth is that the worst possible thing you can do, in terms of personal finance, is to allow a foreclosure to occur. The reason is that the foreclosure could preclude you from getting financing on another house for a long time in the future.

"Isn't that a bit harsh?" you may be saying. After all, if a person goes through bankruptcy, after a few years of steady and on-time paying of bills, he or she can usually get a credit card and start establishing good credit for loans. In many cases the bankruptcy itself is taken off the books after 7 years.

Perhaps. But mortgage lenders are not credit card lenders. They have a different mentality, and they have memories like elephants. To understand, look at it from their perspective for a moment.

Say you loan a friend $1000, and she agrees to repay it with interest.

However, she runs into hard times. She isn't able to make the payments for a while. But she struggles and struggles and eventually pays you back every dime, not including the interest.

Now she wants to borrow again. Will you lend to her?

I would. This is a gal who will keep her bond. Even though things might not work out the way she plans, I'll feel confident that I'll get my money back eventually.

On the other hand, suppose you have another friend who also borrows $1000. When times get tough for him, he walks away from your loan. He never pays you back.

Now he wants to borrow more money. He says everything is financially great with him, and he'll have no trouble repaying. He'll even pay you extra interest. Will you lend to him?

Not me. I'll never feel secure with this person again. I'll always worry that if times get tough, he'll take the easy way out and forget about my loan.

Mortgage lenders are much the same way. They don't really care as much if you have a bankruptcy or if you don't make payments on your credit cards. They'll sometimes look the other way if you don't pay your telephone bill or your water and electric bills. Just have a few good years of steady payments and they'll forgive all the bad times.

But if they ever find out that you let a house go to foreclosure, most will look askance at the idea of giving you another mortgage. The reasoning here is that foreclosure is not like anything else. Lenders see a mortgage as a commitment on both their part and yours. They will lend you more money than you could ever qualify for otherwise on your income. And they anticipate that you will pay it back honorably, no matter what.

TRAP—YOU'LL DO IT AGAIN

The lender's doctrine: A borrower who can live with one foreclosure can live with another.

All of which is to say that if you ever hope to buy another house in the near future, protect your mortgage credit. Find a way to pay off the mortgage. Get yourself off the hook. Don't even consider walking. If you do, you'll find it very difficult to get another mortgage.

Of course, this is not to say that you won't ever be able to get any kind of mortgage. Some lender may get desperate and give you a loan. And there are always the "equity lenders" who will lend a smaller (around 65 percent) percentage of a property's value and don't care who's applying for the loan. Some of them don't even conduct a credit check. (Some actually hope that you won't make payments so that they can foreclose!)

But equity lenders require you to make a huge down payment and charge much higher interest. They are a poor alternative.

TRAP—DON'T THINK YOU CAN SNEAK BY A LENDER

Every mortgage loan application asks if you have *ever* had a foreclosure. Today, most also ask if you have ever given a deed in lieu of foreclosure (which is considered bad, but not nearly as bad as foreclosure).

If you fudge on the application, the foreclosure could show up on a credit report. (Mortgage lenders use the most sophisticated nationwide credit reporting systems available.) Even if it doesn't show up and you do get the loan, should you later default and it turns out that you lied on your application, you could be liable for serious penalties.

TRAP—YOU COULD BE HELD PERSONALLY LIABLE FOR THE MORTGAGE

Usually it's only the property that's collateral for the mortgage. However, unless you obtained the mortgage as part of the purchase price and only in those states that have "purchase money mortgage" laws, even if you walk, the lender could go to court and obtain a deficiency judgment against you personally for any money it loses by taking the property back. This judgment would follow you.

Avoid the Mortgage Credit Trap

In most cases it is possible to avoid foreclosure. It may not be easy. You may need to change your plans or to take actions that you'd rather avoid. You may even have to sell an item that you love, like a boat or a car, to raise money for mortgage payments. You may have to do things that you disdain, like borrowing from relatives. But where there's a will, there's a way. And this is one case where finding the way will bring you a much happier future.

Being upside down is distinctly unpleasant. But don't ever give up hope. There are almost always ways out. You just have to hunt to find them.

14
Financing the Sale Yourself

When you sell your house, you get cash out, right? Of course, you have to pay off your existing mortgage, but the buyers arrange their own financing, right?

That's usually the way it works in today's marketplace. But not always. Sometimes you, the seller, will finance the sale yourself. You'll give the buyer a new mortgage (first, second, or other) and carry back paper. You'll get monthly mortgage payments, and you'll still hold a security interest in the property.

Why Finance It Myself?

1. *You can make a deal that otherwise couldn't be made.* Maybe the buyer can't qualify for a large or low-down-payment institutional loan. But, this is the only buyer to come along in quite a long time. And you have a large equity in the property, so you give the buyer a loan and make the deal.

2. *You want the interest.* Often people who are retired and have large amounts of equity in their homes are looking to sell and then put their money to work earning interest for them. But, when interest rates at banks are very low, it's hard to make much money that way. So, they give the seller a mortgage and get an interest rate on it that's two to three times higher than what the bank is offering.

3. *You can get a higher price.* Sometimes buyers are willing to pay more for a property if the seller will finance it. The reason, of

course, is that the seller doesn't charge points or the other large fees that other lenders charge. Thus, the buyer is willing to pay a higher price.

What Is Seller Financing?

When you go into the grocery store and buy a jar of mayonnaise, you normally pay for it in cash. You give the clerk your $1.50 or $2.00 or whatever and take the mayonnaise, and that's the end of the transaction.

Selling real estate is rarely that simple, particularly in today's high-priced market. Very few buyers have enough cash to pay for the purchase of your home. Instead, they plan to finance most of the purchase price (typically 90 percent or more of it).

The usual route for financing is to go to an institutional lender—a bank, a savings and loan, or a mortgage banker. This lender gives the buyer the money in exchange for a trust deed (a variation of a mortgage, but more commonly used) on the property.

The buyer now gives you the money (which you use to pay off your existing mortgage and costs of sale, keeping what remains for yourself), and the deal is made.

However, sometimes the buyers won't or can't go to an institutional lender. Instead, they come to you and say, "Seller, please finance my purchase of your home." They may want you to carry back a second or third mortgage for all or a portion of the purchase price. If you own your home free and clear, they may even want you to carry back a first mortgage.

With seller financing, you receive "paper" (a mortgage or a trust deed) instead of cash for your sale. Of course, the real question for you, the seller, is: Should I do it? Should I finance my property for the buyer?

Whenever someone wants me to do something, I'm usually wary. Why would the buyer want me to carry back a mortgage?

Typically the reasons are all bad—for you. Here are a few.

Reasons Buyers Want You to Carry the Financing

1. The buyers have bad credit and can't get an institutional loan.

2. The buyers can't qualify (don't have enough income) to get an institutional loan for enough money to make the purchase.

3. The buyers don't have enough cash for the down payment.

4. Interest rates are so high that the buyers can't qualify for a mortgage.

5. The buyers are investors, and they are looking to get a better deal by having you carry the financing.

Seller Financing Example 1

Ann had a house in Las Vegas, Nevada. This was a booming area, and builders were putting up thousands of homes. That was both good and bad. It allowed people to move in easily. But, it made it very difficult to sell a home that you already owned. Ann had been trying to sell her home for some time, without much luck.

So Ann told her agent that she was willing to carry all the down payment in the form of paper. A buyer would have to pay only closing costs to move in.

The agent acknowledged that that would help and quickly found a buyer, who purchased for nothing down, with Ann carrying the paper.

Ann's "paper" was in the form of a second mortgage for the 20 percent down. The first mortgage was an 80 percent mortgage for the balance from a lender. Ann was to receive payments of $200 a month for 5 years on her paper. After that time, the buyer would owe her a balloon payment of $20,000. It seemed like a good deal to her, and so she signed and closed the deal.

Things went well for a few months, but then she stopped getting her $200 monthly payment. She called the buyers, and they said they had both lost their jobs. They would pay her as soon as they found new work.

Ann waited for 3 months. However, when she called back, she discovered that the phone had been disconnected. She flew to Las Vegas (having since moved to Los Angeles) and was shocked to discover that her home was vacant. The new buyers had simply packed up and left. Worse, vandals had broken in and severely damaged it, to the tune of around $5000.

Ann called the agent who had handled the sale and asked him what she should do. He gave her two rather bleak options:

1. She could begin foreclosure proceedings and take back the property. However, to do so, she would have to make up the back payments on the first mortgage (several thousand dollars at that point—the buyers hadn't been paying on the first mortgage either) and pay foreclosure costs, another few thousand or so. Once she got the house back in her name, it would probably cost her another $5000 to fix it up and put it into good enough shape to make another attempt at reselling.

2. She could simply walk away from the property as the buyers had done and *lose all of her second mortgage.*

Ann immediately ruled out option 2. She wasn't going to lose all of her second mortgage. She began foreclosure proceedings, and after several months she got the home back in her name. Then she repaired it. The total costs were around $15,000. (Her second mortgage had been for only $25,000.)

She put the home back on the market, but she was again faced with the same problem: It was hard to sell unless she offered terms. She didn't want to go that route again, so she took it off the market and rented it, waiting for the price to appreciate or the market for existing homes to improve sufficiently for her to sell and make up all her lost costs.

The point of Ann's story is that if you carry back paper on a house in order to make a deal, sometimes you end up with a deal that it would have been better not to have made. There's a definite risk involved.

The reason goes back to the motivations of buyers. Top-notch buyers, those who have credit and cash, often don't need seller financing. They have the cash for a down payment to keep their payments low, and they don't have problems qualifying for a mortgage.

On the other hand, problem buyers who don't have cash or who can't get new financing are looking for seller financing. Thus, sometimes sellers who carry back paper are in reality getting problem buyers, people who can't (or won't) keep up the property or make the payments. These may be people who already have such bad credit that they don't mind walking away if things get rough.

Be Wary of Speculators

There's another category of buyers—speculators. A spate of "get rich quick in real estate" seminars and books has spawned a group of so-called investors whose whole attitude seems to be "I can get rich in real estate by taking advantage of sellers." These people often buy property with seller financing, then refinance the property under the seller's loan to get out what cash they can and leave. The poor seller is stuck in a position even worse than Ann's, for now the property has additional financing on it, frequently for far more than it's worth!

Seller Financing Example 2

This is not to say that all seller financing turns out badly. Sometimes, depending on your motivation for using it, it can turn out quite well.

Chuck was about to retire. He had social security, but he wasn't sure that it would be enough for him to live on during his retirement. He wanted another source of income. His biggest asset was the equity in his home, which was all paid off. Chuck's goal was to sell his home, put the money he received in the bank, and live off the interest.

However, the bank's highest interest rate at the time was around 2 percent. Since Chuck would get about $250,000 from the sale of his home, that meant that he would receive roughly $5000 a year. He needed a lot more than that.

When it came time to sell, the agent suggested that instead of looking for a buyer who would get a new institutional loan, Chuck should carry the first mortgage. Firsts were then paying about 6 percent interest, which would translate into about $15,000 a year in income for him. In addition, if he made the loan for 20 years, he could be fairly well assured of a steady income for a long time to come.

Chuck thought it was a good idea.

When buyers were found, the agent qualified them just as if they were getting a new institutional loan. They had to have good credit, they had to have sufficient income to "qualify" (roughly three times the monthly payment after all long-term debt, such as car payments), and they had to have at least a 10 percent down payment.

The buyers purchased, and Chuck carried back the financing. It's been nearly 6 years now, and Chuck's monthly check hasn't been late once.

Why Two Different Outcomes?

A large part of the reason for Chuck's success and Ann's failure has to do with their motivation for carrying back paper. In Ann's case, she felt that it was the only way to make a sale. Consequently, she was willing to accept less than desirable buyers (or at least not to properly qualify them).

In Chuck's case, however, the motivation was long-term income. Chuck was willing to sell only to buyers who were totally qualified.

TIP—KNOW YOUR
MOTIVATION

Be aware of your motives when you carry back paper. If you're desperate to sell and you use seller financing to attract a buyer, be aware that you may get a less-than-desirable buyer. You might even end up losing more than you gain by making the sale.

Some savvy sellers use seller financing in the hopes of increasing their profits on the sale. Sometimes these are unscrupulous deals.

The Seller Who Outsmarts
the Bad Buyer

Here, the seller's goal is to sell the property to a buyer in hopes that the buyer will default after a year or so and that the seller can get the property back through foreclosure. In this way, the seller can keep reselling the same property over and over!

There are two catches here. First, the sellers have to keep their costs down. These sellers typically sell FSBO, on their own, so that they don't have any commission to pay. Their only expenses are the closing costs when they sell and the foreclosure costs later on when they take the property back.

Second, they get a large enough down payment from the buyers to cover all their costs plus a profit.

Since it's often a year or more before the buyers default and the sellers foreclose, they hope that the market price of the home will go up. If it does, that means that each time the sellers get the property back, they are able to resell it for a higher price!

I'm not advocating this approach. I'm simply mentioning it to point out that if you want to play the game as a seller, you can play it to win.

The Seller Who Converts Paper into Cash

Paper can be converted to cash, depending on a number of variables. Here's how sellers can take advantage of this conversion.

The sellers have a house to sell that they feel is worth $200,000 on the market in a cash deal. They put it up for sale at $210,000 and offer to take partial paper.

Buyers presumably are willing to pay a little more for the house, since they don't have to put up a cash down payment. The deal is made. The buyers move in and begin making payments to the seller on a second mortgage.

The seller waits at least 6 months, during which time the buyer (hopefully) makes regular monthly payments on the second mortgage. Then the seller sells that second mortgage to a buyer of seconds for cash. The seller ends up with a cash profit.

The advantage of this sale is that the seller, hopefully, is able to move the house faster by offering to carry back some of the paper than by waiting for an all-cash buyer, and also makes some extra money.

Why the 6-month wait?

I'm sure some readers are wondering why the seller waited 6 months before converting the second mortgage to cash.

Indeed, the seller could have converted that note to cash in escrow, and this is sometimes done. However, buyers of second notes (investors who are looking to get higher interest on their cash) are wary of "unseasoned" seconds. They don't know whether the buyer will actually make the payments or will simply default. Buyers of seconds normally don't want to get involved in foreclosure.

If you sell a second mortgage in escrow, the buyer of that second will normally pay less than if you let it "age" for a minimum of 6 months. Our seller waited 6 months to be sure that he got top dollar (around 80 percent of the face value) for selling the second.

Why only 80 percent of face value?

A second question many readers are sure to be asking is, why didn't the buyer of the second pay the full face value of the second in cash? Why was there a 20 percent discount?

The reason has to do with yield and risk. Yield is the actual percentage rate of interest that a buyer of mortgages gets. It is computed through a fairly complex formula that takes into account the interest rate, the amount of cash paid out, and the term.

Yield Example

A second mortgage for 3 years may have a stated interest rate of 12 percent. However, because of the risk of foreclosure in the second-mortgage market, an investor may demand a yield of 18 percent. How does he or she get that yield from a 12 percent mortgage? The answer is by discounting the second mortgage. A 12 percent mortgage that pays $15,000 at maturity, but that costs the buyer of that mortgage only $10,000 in cash, will in fact yield upward of 18 percent interest. (The 18 percent is figured on the $10,000 that was actually invested.)

Thus, by discounting the second mortgage, the seller is able to find an investor who is willing to buy it for cash.

TIP—MAKE IT A BIG SECOND

The trick with offers to carry back a second mortgage with the intention of converting it to cash is to get a large enough second. You need to have enough leeway so that when you sell the mortgage at a discount, you get out the cash you want.

What makes a second mortgage salable?

Finally, it's important to understand that simply taking back a second mortgage as part of seller financing doesn't guarantee that you can resell it. Here's what investors are looking for in seconds.

What Second-Mortgage Buyers Look For

1. A high interest rate. The higher the better.

2. A short term, preferably under 5 years. However, very short terms mean that the investor has to turn his or her money around too often. Longer terms mean that the money is tied up against an uncertain future, where interest rate fluctuations could reduce the value of the second.

3. A late penalty. This is important. The second should contain a money penalty if the buyers are more than a couple of weeks late with their payment. The reason is simple: If there is no penalty,

then each time the buyers are late, the holder of the second has only one option—to start foreclosure, which is an expensive proposition. On the other hand, if the second has a penalty, it is easy to enforce and encourages prompt payment.

4. Proper documents. Improper documents or documents that are improperly executed account for more failures of seconds than people realize. If you're giving a second as part of the sale, be sure you have a competent attorney check out the documents.

What about Balloon Payments?

Finally, there is the matter of balloon payments on second mortgages. Often second mortgages will have a final payment, called a "balloon," that is much higher than all the other payments. This is done when the interest rate is too low or the term is too short to allow the buyer to pay off the mortgage.

If all goes well, this will work out fine for the seller. At the end of the term of the mortgage, say 4 years, the buyers will refinance and fully pay off the seller. You get your monthly payments *and* your final payoff!

Sometimes, however, it doesn't go smoothly.

At the end of the short term of the second mortgage, the buyers normally have to refinance to get enough cash to pay off the balloon. However, if for financial reasons they can't refinance, then they can't pay it off. And the seller could be left holding the bag.

For this reason, at the end of the second mortgage term, many sellers will offer to extend the mortgage for an additional term of years at the then current interest rate. In this way, the seller preserves capital while receiving a good interest rate on it.

Checklist for Seller Financing

	YES	NO
1. Are you getting the current market interest rate for seconds?	[ ]	[ ]

Check with agents, with the local paper under ads for seconds for sale, and with mortgage brokers to find the current rate.

	YES	NO
2. Are you giving the right term?	[ ]	[ ]

Seconds longer than 5 years are sometimes considered too long-term to be salable.

	YES	NO
3. Have you checked out the buyers' credit?	[ ]	[ ]

You can get a credit report either directly from a credit agency or through your agent. If the buyers have any bad credit at all, you're significantly increasing your risk of having to take the property back.

	YES	NO
4. Have you gotten an estimate of foreclosure costs in your state?	[ ]	[ ]

There are professionals who specialize in handling foreclosures. They often advertise under Real Estate in the classified section of papers. Or you can contact an escrow officer or a real estate agent who can direct you to one. Find out what your costs are likely to be now, before you commit.

	YES	NO
5. Are the buyers putting a lot of cash into the property?	[ ]	[ ]

The more cash the buyers are putting in, the more committed they will be to holding on to the property and avoiding default. Beware of buyers who put no cash down.

	YES	NO
6. Are you careful to *avoid* having a subordination clause in your second?	[ ]	[ ]

A subordination clause makes your second mortgage "subordinate" to another mortgage. What this means is that the buyers could refinance the first mortgage for more money, making your second virtually worthless. Usually avoid this like the plague.

	YES	NO
7. Are your documents correct?	[ ]	[ ]

The only way for you to have any sense of security here is to have your documents examined by (if not prepared by) a competent real estate attorney.

	YES	NO
8. Have you consulted an attorney and a tax planner/ accountant to determine the tax consequences of getting a second mortgage?	[ ]	[ ]

In some cases, even though you got back paper, the government may treat the sale as cash and require you to pay tax on the money that you didn't receive!

	YES	NO
9. Have you consulted with an expert on seller financing in your area to be sure that you're handling the deal correctly?	[ ]	[ ]

Each state has somewhat different laws and rules regarding second mortgages. Be sure you're in compliance with the rules in your state.

15

12 Tools for Getting Your Agent to Work Harder

Usually you don't realize that there's a problem with your agent until a month or more has passed. Then, when you notice that there are no good offers and that few people have been stopping by, you begin wondering what's the problem.

A call to your agent will often produce a variety of responses, such as

"I'm doing everything I can."

"The market's soft right now; just wait."

"Cut your price to get a sale."

None of those answers are what you want to hear. Rather, what you want is some positive feedback telling you that more people will begin looking at your house and that in short order you'll get at least one, and hopefully several, good offers.

How do get your agent to respond in such a manner and mean it?

Here are 12 tools that you can use to light a fire under an agent who isn't really holding up his or her end of the bargain.

Tool 1: Agency Promotion

Is the agent promoting your property to the other agents in his or her office?

Agents rarely work alone. Rather, the agent is typically one of many agents, sometimes dozens, in a broker's office. It seems only natural, therefore, that your agent should promote your home to other agents in the same office. But, has it happened?

Ask your agent if he or she has physically handed the listing to all the other agents in the office. What about sending emails on the listing to every other agent? What about putting up a flyer for the property on the office bulletin board?

There are many ways in which an agent can promote your property to other office agents.

What you don't want is an agent who hides your listing, hoping to find a buyer and thus collect not only the listing commission, but also the buyer's agent's commission. If your agent is the only one looking for a buyer, then the odds that a buyer will be found are small. But if dozens of agents from the same office are looking, the odds get much better.

Ask to be sent copies of the flyers sent to other office agents. Ask to be copied on emails sent. Ask if you can come in and talk to other agents yourself to promote your house. Remember, the more agents there are at work on selling your property, the quicker the sale.

Tool 2: Cobroking

Is the agent promoting your property to agents in other offices?

You want your agent to be promoting your home to all other offices as well as his or her own office. There might be a thousand agents in your area. You want every one of them to know about your house. You want them to be eager to show it.

**TRAP—DON'T LET
YOUR AGENT JUST
MLS YOUR PROPERTY**

Don't accept the fact that your agent has put your home on the Multiple Listing Service as sufficient. Yes, that makes it available to other agents, but it doesn't get them fired up about it. There might be 5000 other homes in your area for sale on the MLS at any given time. What's to distinguish yours?

Consider how the "system" works from the buyer's perspective. The vast majority of buyers seek out agents to find the right home for them. They know that the great preponderance of homes are listed. Therefore, it's only sensible for them to look with the aid of an agent.

You're listed with an agent, and potential buyers are looking with agents. All that's needed is for your agent to contact the right buyer's agent, and a deal can be made.

Tool 3: Caravanning

Has your agent organized broker caravans? With a broker caravan, agents from one or many offices all come by to see a (usually new) listing. If a picture is worth a thousand words, then actually seeing the property is worth a million. An agent who's actually been out to your home will remember it and will tend to think of it when working with buyers.

Did your agent organize an office caravan? Did your agent organize an interoffice caravan? If she or he did, you would know it.

If your agent didn't do this, contact him or her about doing it. Ask about having a second and even a third caravan.

Tool 4: Broker's Open House

Beware of agents who are eager to hold an "open house." With an open house, the agent sticks a sign out front on a Sunday afternoon saying that your house is open to anyone who wants to look, then sits there waiting.

The problem is that the agent isn't waiting for a buyer for your home. He or she is waiting for a buyer (or seller) for some other home. Studies have repeatedly shown that people who show up at an open house rarely buy that property. However, they often hook up with the agent sitting there and end up buying a different piece of property.

Therefore, it rarely does you any good to have a traditional open house.

On the other hand, it does worlds of good to have a "broker's open house." With this type of open house, the public is not invited. Only other agents are invited.

Typically a broker's open house is held mid-morning on a weekday, and if your agent is any good at all, he or she will offers food (coffee cake, sandwiches, cookies, or something similar) and drink (coffee, champagne, or orange juice, for example). It may sound silly, but my experience has been that if you offer food and drink, the agents will come in droves to look at your home. And once they see it, as noted earlier, they are likely to remember it and promote it.

**TIP—OFFER TO HELP
PAY FOR THE
REFRESHMENTS**

Agents are on really tight budgets. If you offer to pop for $50 or $100 for the broker's open house, it's much more likely to happen. Yes, it costs you a little bit extra, but it could make for a much quicker sale at a better price.

Tool 5: Refill the Flyer Box

It should go without saying that your broker should provide flyers in a little box to go on your "For Sale" sign out front. Often, however, the flyers go in the first week. And then, after neighbors have taken them, the box stays empty.

An empty flyer box does you no good in helping to sell your home. Therefore, keep after the agent to refill the box. A good agent will come at least once a week, preferably on a Friday (before the buyers come by looking on the weekend), to refill the box.

If your agent balks at this simple task, then do it yourself. After all, chances are you're there all the time anyhow. Get copies made up, and be sure that the flyer box is filled all the time.

Tool 6: Better Sign Placement

Of course your agent put a sign up in your yard. If you've got a small yard facing the street, then the sign is undoubtedly facing forward, stuck in the front yard.

The question to ask yourself is, can motorists driving by see the sign from a distance? Or are they past it before they actually realize it's there?

Better sign placement may help promote your property. Here are some ideas to consider with your agent.

Good Sign Placements

- Double signs, back to back, so that people driving by in either direction can see them
- Two signs on a corner lot
- Two signs on a wide lot, one at each side
- A bigger, bolder sign
- Signs on adjoining property (where allowed) directing buyers to your home

**TRAP—BEWARE OF
SIGN RESTRICTIONS**

Some neighborhoods restrict the size, appearance, and placement of signs. If that's the case in your neighborhood, you can seek an exception, but don't count on getting it.

Tool 7: Better Communication

A good agent has an ethical responsibility to keep you informed. That means that the agent calls you regularly, perhaps weekly, to let you know what he or she has done recently to sell your home.

Not only is this good business practice, but it may also help with the sale, since during those conversations you may be able to suggest sales approaches that the agent didn't think of. If your agent doesn't call you frequently, call your agent and demand to know what's going on.

Tool 8: Buyer Bargains

What makes your home stand out from all the others?

What can your agent do for you at meetings when he or she "talks up" your house to other agents?

Your agent can stand up at a listing meeting and say, "I've got a house here that will knock your socks off. And my seller has reduced the price to help you get buyers excited about this property." (Even a small reduction is noteworthy.)

Or your agent can say, "My seller has said, bring me any reasonable offer!" (You surely did say that, didn't you?)

Or your agent can say, "My seller is offering to throw in the appliances and the refrigerator" (which you were willing to leave anyhow).

You get the idea. Your agent's best weapon is spreading the word around, and anything you can do to help your agent get other agents excited about your property (such as reducing the price, offering better terms, or offering actual bonuses) only helps.

Tool 9: Agent Bonuses

Do you want to really catch the attention of other agents? Offer them a bonus.

Your agent stands up at a listing meeting (or sends an email out) and says, "My seller is offering an extra $500 (or $1000) to the agent who brings in a buyer!" The bonus could also be free tickets to a highly prized ball game, tickets to a vacation resort, appliances, or almost anything else.

I guarantee that this will make other agents prick up their ears. No, it's not going to enable them to make buyers materialize out of thin air. But if there's a buyer who's remotely interested in a home like yours, they will show it to him or her and try to get him or her to buy.

Sometimes it's the little things that make the big difference. A few hundred dollars on the sale of a home is peanuts, compared with getting a fast sale for a big price. (Besides, you don't pay the bonus unless and until the house sells!)

Tool 10: Increase Advertising

Just as buyers who attend open houses rarely buy that house, as noted earlier, studies have repeatedly shown that buyers rarely purchase the home they call about in response to an advertisement. They buy some other house. However, that doesn't mean that a buyer who calls about some other house won't buy yours!

The agent may not be advertising your house per se, but the agent's office should have a stream of advertising running constantly in all the local media (newspapers, magazines, movie theaters, and so on). It's even better if the advertising is for homes in the same price range and style as yours.

Some sellers insist on writing into their listing agreements that the agent will spend X dollars on advertising. The hope is that if the agent commits to a large enough figure for advertising the property, then he or she will push the property.

Maybe that works and maybe it doesn't. Most good agents I know won't agree to a set advertising figure on a specific home. They know that it's just wasted money and that it reduces their commission.

Tool 11: Online Listing

In today's world, your home should definitely be listed online. Most homes that are on the MLS end up on realtor.com, which is cosponsored by the National Association of Realtors. However, your broker may also have his or her own web site. And there may be other good real estate web sites in your area.

In truth, few sales come directly from web sites. However, once a buyer spots your home by driving by, he or she may be encouraged by the flyer (in a box on the sign, remember?) to go to a web site and get much more detailed information.

From there, it takes only an email or a phone call to contact the broker. And your house sale could be on its way.

Tool 12: Break the Bad Listing

Thus far, we've look at ways of helping and encouraging your agent to help get you a buyer. But sometimes things are beyond that.

Usually a serious problem doesn't develop until after the first month. But then, if no buyers come by; there are no ads in the paper, no caravans, and no open houses; and you can't contact your agent (or you get an insufficient answer to your question), you may discover that you've got what I call a Lister Only.

A Lister Only is an agent who takes a listing, puts it on the MLS, and forgets about it. He or she hopes that someone else will sell it. If no one does, then too bad. This agent is on to getting more listings.

TRAP—THOSE WHO LIST, LAST!

That's an old saying that some real estate agents live by: Forget about everything else—just get enough listings, and you'll have a successful real estate career. Of course, the agent's not promoting your property doesn't help you, the seller.

If you believe that your agent really isn't working on your property, call or go in to see her or him. Instead of showing anger, show concern. Explain that you haven't seen any results and, after all, results are what listing and selling are all about. Give the agent an opportunity to explain, and listen carefully to the explanation.

Does the explanation make sense? Has the agent talked up your house all over town? Was the agent just too busy to call you and let you know? (Remember, a good agent will always find time to call and keep you informed.) Are caravans, broker's open houses, and other tools in the works?

If the agent seems sincere about changing his or her ways, or explains that he or she just hasn't communicated everything that he or she is doing for you, give the agent a second chance. If you are near the beginning or middle of the listing period, give the agent another 2 weeks. See what happens.

If, after a second chance, the agent still refuses to work on your property, and you have only a few more weeks left on the listing, common sense suggests that you wait it out. The listing will soon expire, and you can go elsewhere.

What If I Have a Long-Term Listing?

On the other hand, if you've signed a long-term listing (remember, I suggest a maximum of 3 months), you can demand to have your listing back. Say that you're unsatisfied with the agent's work and you want to list your property elsewhere.

TRAP—YOU CAN'T ARBITRARILY CANCEL YOUR LISTING

When you sign a listing for a set period of time, generally speaking, you cannot take back your listing unless the agent agrees. Some listing agreements contain a "liquidated damages" clause. Beware of this clause. It often states that if for any reason you decide to take your house off the market, you owe the agent whatever commission was written in there.

How Do I Get My Listing Back?

If your agent refuses to release your listing, then go to the agent's broker. Explain that you're very unhappy with this agent who isn't working on your property. Ask if the broker will transfer the listing to another agent in the office.

To avoid hard feelings and ameliorate a bad situation, the broker may be willing to "encourage" your old agent to agree to a transfer. If that's the case, then interview agents (as discussed in Chapter 4) to be sure that you don't get another ringer.

If the broker won't act, you can next go to the local real estate board (both your broker and your agent are very likely to be members). However, don't expect a sympathetic hearing. After all, who can really say what constitutes working with diligence on a listing?

When All Else Fails

Here are several ways to pressure your agent to release your listing:

1. If your agent is a salesperson, tell her or him that you are going to complain to the broker. If this doesn't do any good, go to see the broker and state your case as noted earlier.
2. Tell your agent that you are quite angry and that you are going to file a written complaint with the local real estate board and the

state real estate licensing department. Quite frankly, since it's a matter of judgment, neither of these steps is likely to produce much in the way of results. But most agents would rather not have letters of complaint registered against them, particularly with the state. Show the agent the letters. If this doesn't move the agent, send the letters on with a copy to the agent.

3. Tell the agent that you're going to complain in writing to the local chamber of commerce, the Better Business Bureau, or even the district attorney. Show the letters to the agent before you send them. If the agent doesn't become agreeable to what you want, send the letters. Again, since it's a judgment call, don't expect big results.

4. Tell your agent that you're going to write a letter of complaint to your local newspaper. This is a no-win situation for the agent. There's always a chance that your letter of complaint will end up in the letters-to-the-editor department. That will draw public attention to the problem—a powerful tactic. If you've already said that you were going to send letters (as described earlier) and then you actually did send them, the agent will surely believe that you'll send this one. And who knows what letters local newspapers (which are traditionally hungry for any news at all to fill their pages) will print. If the agent doesn't go along, send the letter—just be sure that your letter states facts and does *not* contain any slander or libelous statements.

Notice that all of these tactics have two parts. First, you tell the agent what you are going to do and give him or her a chance to respond. If the agent doesn't agree to give you back your listing, then you do it. The steps also follow in sequence from lesser to greater pressure.

The point is that, in reality, there's probably nothing specific that you can do. All that you can hope for is to convince the agent that you're sufficiently mad about what the agent has (or has not) done that it's easier and better just to give back the listing. After awhile you become a nuisance, and the agent may give you back your listing just to get rid of your complaining.

What happens if your agent is a real stinker and isn't moved by any of this?

Hopefully you didn't sign a really long listing, and by the time you've tried all of these maneuvers, the listing period will be almost up anyway. Just wait it out and get a better agent next time.

16

12 Tips When Selling Condos, Co-Ops, and Townhouses

The big questions that sellers usually ask when they're selling a condo, co-op, or townhome is, are there any special differences? There are, and then again, there aren't. Here's what to pay special attention to.

Tip 1: Get a Sign Out

With a single-family home, one of the best methods of advertising (if not *the* best) is to put a "For Sale" sign in the front yard. Since the front yard of a condo is owned by everyone in the association, you normally can't do that. In fact, most condominium bylaws preclude you from putting a "For Sale" sign for your condo in any common area. Thus, letting people know that you have a condo for sale can be difficult. But it's not impossible.

First, use an agent. It's much harder to sell a condo FSBO than it is to sell a single-family house. The agent can meet buyers at the office and then bring them by. This makes a having a sign less compelling.

Second, see if you can fudge on the sign. Try putting a sign in the window of your unit or on the garage door. If you face the street, you might be able to get lots of exposure. Besides, most people won't complain about this. Chances are no one will say anything about it, at least initially.

TRAP—THE RULES MAY PROHIBIT USING ANY SIGN AT ALL

Some condominium homeowner associations (HOAs) and co-op boards (condos have homeowner associations; co-ops have boards of directors) prohibit you from even putting a sign on the exterior walls, on the doors, or in the windows of your own unit. Such rules can be hard to enforce and perhaps even illegal, but strict homeowner associations and boards may try to enforce them.

TIP—A TOWNHOUSE IS USUALLY A CONDO

Legally speaking, a townhouse is simply a condominium where the owners own the land beneath their unit and the sky above. This is as opposed to a traditional condo, where the owners own only the airspace. Thus, a townhouse is more a description of a shape than a legal entity. (Note: It is possible to have co-ops in the shape of a townhouse.)

Tip 2: Arrange for Showing

With a single-family home, showing simply means having buyers come by and take a look. If you're not home, a lockbox on the house can allow agents with buyers to gain access.

With a condo or a co-op, however, you often must get permission to get through a gate or door. This means that unless you want to give everyone the code for the gate (or a pass for the door), you must arrange for showings. Thus, it will take more time to show a condo or co-op for you or your agent.

Plan on spending lots of weekends trying to sell your unit. It's undoubtedly going to take more time and effort than selling a single-family home.

Tip 3: Have CC&RS and Bylaws Available

Condos and co-ops are not simply less expensive and smaller single-family homes. They are actually a different type of lifestyle, a shared lifestyle.

It's important that each buyer who comes by understands this, and the best way to make sure that buyers do understand is to have a set of bylaws and CC&Rs (deed conditions, covenants, and restrictions) available. That way, buyers can see what you're actually offering.

**TRAP—DON'T LOSE
THE DEAL BECAUSE
BUYERS DIDN'T
KNOW**

 At some point, every buyer will be made aware of the bylaws and CC&Rs, either by the agent or by the HOA or the board. It's better that buyers find out early on and make an educated purchase decision, rather than finding out late and spending a lot of time and aggravation trying to get out of the deal.

Some sellers will offer a short list of the rules of the association or board to help buyers identify the restrictions and the amenities that are offered.

Tip 4: For Co-Ops, Talk to the Board First

A co-op is actually a stock corporation. The board runs it, and your evidence of ownership usually takes the form of stock and a proprietary lease on your unit.

That means that in order to sell, you often have to get the permission of the board. When the board gives permission, it will take back your stock and issue new stock and a new lease to the buyer. Of course, the sale is handled in the usual manner, and you get your equity out, normally in the form of cash.

However, all of this means that the board must give you permission to sell to this buyer. This control is, in fact, one of the factors that may make your co-op more valuable and desirable. Many buyers like being able to have some control over who their neighbors will be.

Of course, such control is more limited today than it was in the past. In general, co-ops today may not limit buyers on the basis of race, religion, health, gender preference, or national origin.

However, many co-ops do restrict buyers on the basis of their income level or their ability to pay their monthly fees. The reason is that the co-op may have a single large mortgage covering the entire building. If one unit owner fails to pay, then the others must make up the difference. Thus, the other members, through the board, have a vested interest in seeing that your buyer is financially sound.

By first talking to the board, or at least the general manager, you will be able to get a sense of what the board is looking for in a new buyer and save yourself from wasting a lot of time and effort by bringing in someone who's not fully qualified.

Tip 5: For Condos, Talk to the Architectural Committee First

With condos, you can generally sell to whomever you please. However, the new owners will have to abide by the general bylaws and other rules governing the development.

Condos are typically very strict about any changes to the property. For example, your unit may lack an interior washer and dryer, and you may want to install one (or suggest to buyers that they may want to install one) as part of an inducement to purchase.

However, the architectural committee may not give its approval. And if it doesn't, you probably won't be able to put in your interior washroom. (Installing an interior washroom could affect the plumbing, which is shared by the other unit owners, or create noise.)

Be sure to check out any issues involving changes before you list your unit. That way you can be prepared to handle questions about such changes from agents and potential buyers.

Tip 6: Give Buyers Detailed Instructions for Getting There

Whether you're selling by owner or through an agent, you can't show a unit unless the buyers can find it. With a single-family house, it's just a matter of giving driving instructions. With a condo or co-op, on the other hand, there's also the matter of finding the unit within the development.

Don't assume that everyone is as good with directions as you are. I've spent more time than I liked wandering around condo developments and co-op buildings, totally lost and unable to find the unit I was searching for. (And I usually have excellent directional instincts!)

The best solution is to create a map of the development and/or building and give to everyone who's interested. You can also put it up on a web site, email it, and fax it.

Tip 7: Always Show with the Lights on High

An old trick when showing homes is to always turn on all the lights. This makes the home appear brighter and more enticing to potential buyers.

This rule is of particular significance to many sellers of condos and co-ops. The reason is that chances are your unit has some access to the outdoors, probably at the front and rear. But if your unit is in a building, it's also very likely that there are solid walls on the sides. This means that, compared to a house, there is only half the opportunity for light from outdoors to penetrate and illuminate the interior.

I can tell you from experience in showing condos that when the owners do not turn on all the lights, buyers almost universally complain about how dark the place is inside—and this on a bright sunny day. For many buyers, it's the difference between making an offer and looking elsewhere.

If your unit is particularly dark, you may even want to go out and purchase extra lamps. You can get very bright inexpensive floor lamps (around $30 a pop) and set them up in every room. It can make all the difference.

Tip 8: Prepare to Explain Lawsuits

Today, it's almost unusual for a condo or co-op not to be involved in lawsuits of one sort or another. Sometimes the owners are suing the building over defects. Other times the board or HOA is suing an owner for failure to pay fees. Or an owner is suing the development over restrictions. Or owners are suing owners over grievances.

These lawsuits present an obstacle to selling your unit. Buyers don't like them, and lenders don't either. The reason is that, depending on who wins and who loses, all the owners in the development might be asked to pay a share of a sometimes sizable judgment. Thus, if you have a lawsuit pending, it could scare away a buyer or make it difficult for that buyer to obtain the necessary financing.

It's important that you disclose all lawsuits to a buyer. This is to protect yourself from that buyer's coming back later and trying to get out of the deal, saying that you withheld important information about your unit. Most boards and HOAs will provide this information to you and your buyer. *Note:* They may not provide the details of the case, but they should be able to provide the names of the parties and other general information of record.

It's a good idea to consult with a member of the board or HOA to learn what's out there and to get some background on it. Thus, when your buyer is alarmed about a lawsuit that the board has against the builder, you can explain that it's over leaking roofs and that the insurance will cover most of it, but that the board is trying to recover the deductible, or whatever.

Tip 9: Be Ready to Explain Your Neighbors

With a single-family house, the neighbors are some distance away, and even if they are loud and raucous, you can usually live with them (see Chapter 6). With many condos and co-ops, however, the neighbors are as close as a next-door apartment. Loud noises in particular can be a problem.

It's a good idea to disclose to buyers any problem neighbors that you have. And put your disclosure in writing. That way, the buyers can't come back to you after the sale and say that you never told them.

Yes, this could scare some buyers away. On the other hand, it could make the deal you do get stick.

Tip 10: Explain the Lifestyle

Try to be there when buyers come by. By all means show them your unit. But then take them on a tour of the development.

If you have these amenities, or any others, show them off:

- Swimming pool and spa
- Tennis courts
- Golf putting range
- Clubhouse
- Exercise room

If possible, point out how close your unit is to these facilities.

Sometimes buyers may decide to make a purchase not because they fall in love with your unit, but because they like the extra features that your development offers. Sometimes they'll buy in spite of your unit in order to get the amenities!

Tip 11: Help with the Financing

If the buyers are having some difficulty getting financing for your unit, offer to carry some of the paper yourself. (See Chapter 14 for how to do this.)

As noted earlier, buyers may have difficulty finding a lender if the development has lots of lawsuits. They may also have difficulty if more than 25 percent of the development is rented out. Lenders often steer clear of condos and co-ops that have a higher rental-to-owner ratio than 1 to 4. They figure that there's too much turnover and too much chance that owners are renting because they can't sell—not a good spot to place a loan.

However, what lenders may be willing to do is offer financing for 70 or 80 percent of the value. (This is as opposed to the up to 100 percent that is commonly available to qualified buyers.)

Thus, you would need to offer a second mortgage for perhaps 10 to 20 percent or more of the purchase price. Assuming that you have enough equity to do this, you would get your money out in the form of paper instead of cash. (Again, check into Chapter 14 for ways of converting paper to cash.)

Tip 12: Help with the Sale

Finally, if the market for condos and co-ops in your area is not particularly strong, your agent may not be willing to spend enough resources on your unit to get a sale. You may find that this isn't just a failing of a particular agent, but rather is the general mindset of all agents in the area. Yes, they'll take your listing. However, they figure it won't sell, so they aren't willing to push it.

If this is the case, you may need to do all the things suggested in Chapter 15. In addition, you may want to spend your own money on your own advertising campaign. To compensate, you may want to look for a fee-for-service broker or a discount broker.

Of course, when the market is strong, these problems rarely surface, and a sale should be made quickly and for a good price.

17

Five
Troubleshooting
Keys When It
Won't Sell

The first question you're probably going to ask is why this chapter has only five techniques when the previous two chapters have 12.

While there is a tremendous impulse to make things symmetrical, and I had indeed originally titled this chapter "12 Techniques. . . ," I found that there really were only five. Furthermore, these five are so important that I didn't want any sellers to miss them by diluting them.

So, here are the five techniques that are key to getting you a sale quickly and for more money.

Technique 1: Help the Neighborhood

As sellers, how can we offer buyers a better neighborhood? Or can we?

Obviously, you can't move your house to a better neighborhood. However, there are some things that you can do to improve the neighborhood around you. And you can sometimes expand a potential buyer's perspective on the true quality of your area.

A few years ago, a friend of mine had a home in a rather rundown area that he was trying to sell. To make things worse, neighbors across the street were in the habit of working on their cars on their front lawn.

Potential buyers would drive up to my friend's house, only to see the mess across the street. Most of them wouldn't even stop; they'd just drive on.

After many months, my friend sold his property for far less than he had put into it. He virtually gave it away.

The new owner was an investor. She immediately put the house back up for sale. Then she went across the street to the bad neighbors, knocked on the door, and asked a favor.

She said, "I'm trying to teach my son responsibility and how to do a good job. I wonder if you'd mind if he came over and mowed your lawn? It'll be a good experience for him." The neighbor was astonished and looked across the street to a perfectly manicured lawn. "Sure," the neighbor said. "Why not?"

"Fine," she said, "How soon can you move the car?"

The neighbor was taken aback. But something clicked. She says it was embarrassment at the appearance of the home. Soon afterward, the cars were moved into the garage, and every week her son went over to mow the lawn, trim the bushes, and sometimes even water. The neighbor felt that he was getting a good deal. And the investor never mentioned the $15 a week she was paying her son.

Others in the neighborhood, who were relieved to see the mess cleaned up, began complimenting the bad neighbor, who felt even better about that. Soon other neighbors also cleaned up their front yards. And the neighbor with the messy lawn soon began improving his house as well.

She resold that home within a few months for a substantial profit. Nothing will pop up the price of a home faster than neighborhood improvement.

Improve the Perception of the Neighborhood

Even if you do improve the look of the homes on your street, you can't give your home a Beverly Hills address unless it's in Beverly Hills—or can you?

I once had a home that was in a modest area, but near the border of a highly desired area. When I advertised my property, did I say that I was in the modest area? Or did my ad say "next to" the more desired neighborhood?

Furthermore, when potential buyers who stop by are wary of the area, you can make an effort to demonstrate that your neighborhood is greatly underrated. You can point out that few people realize that you have a park nearby, that you are close to shopping, that you have great access to freeways, that you have greenbelts, that your school's test scores are way up, or whatever. In other words, your neighborhood is actually far better than it is commonly perceived as being.

You can also explain that people are just now discovering the true value of your neighborhood. Why, within a year or two, yours could be among the most desired in the county, perhaps the state. The purchaser of your home may be getting in cheap, before people in general realize how desirable an area it really is and prices go up.

Will buyers believe it? If it's close enough to the truth, many will.

TIP—IT'S THE SIZZLE
THAT COUNTS

For most people, the perception is more important than the reality, the sizzle more mouthwatering than the steak. As long as buyers perceive that you're in a desirable neighborhood, it doesn't matter how good or bad your area really is.

Technique 2: Offer a Better Price

How can I get my price and offer a good value to the buyer too?

You don't have to give the buyer a good price in order to sell your home. You just have to offer a realistic price.

The hardest thing for most sellers to accept is price realism. When you're selling, whether what you're selling is T-shirts, bananas, or houses, you're in competition with others who are selling the same or very similar products. If the vendor down the road is selling bananas for 67 cents a pound, how many people do you think will pay you $1.02 a pound? They'll say, "Why should I pay more? I'll go down the street and get the same bananas for less." It's the same with houses.

In order for your house to sell, your price must be competitive. If you ask more than the market will bear, even just a few thousand dollars more, it'll take you much longer to sell even in a strong market, and you may never sell in a slow market.

TRAP—DON'T GET HUNG UP ON PRICE

 A property is worth just what a buyer will pay for it, and no more. The hard truth is that it makes no difference how much you paid for it, how much you owe on it, or how much you put into it. Only the market determines the price.

Getting a Better Price

This having been said, it's important for you to understand that you can indeed get a better price for your house than your neighbor got for his or hers *if* you can convince a buyer that yours is a superior product. The reason that you're charging $1.02 for your bananas is that they are organically grown. Or they are bigger. Or they taste better. Some buyers who are looking for a superior product will pay your higher price.

In other words, if you can convince buyers that your house is in some way superior to seemingly comparable homes that are selling for less, you can get more. The difficulty is convincing the buyers of this, as they are very savvy these days. Remember, buyers shop neighborhood first. Thus, they already have a good idea of what your house should be worth, given its location, even before they stop by.

Nevertheless, within every neighborhood there's a price *range*. You want to be at the top of the range, not at the bottom or even near the middle. What can you do to accomplish this?

You can't change the size of your house. If you have 1500 square feet, you can't make it into 1800. (Unless you add on, but that might mean that you're overbuilding for your neighborhood, and you might get only 50 cents on the dollar for what it costs to do the work.) And you can't move your home to a better locale.

But you can "doll up" your house. You can make its appearance so irresistible that a buyer will perceive that it is a better product and be willing to pay more for your home than for the "dog" that your neighbor down the street is selling for less.

Technique 3: Improve Your Home's Appearance

There's an enormous amount that you can do (check back in Chapter 2 for details). But for now, let's assume that there's nothing drastically wrong with your home (no holes in the walls, no broken floors, no caved-in roof, and so on). Here are the four most important, inexpensive, and quick cosmetic improvements that you can make.

Four Best Improvements to Make to Get a Quick Sale

1. Fix the Driveway
A driveway takes up an enormous amount of the front of your home. It's what people usually see first when they drive up. It's often what they walk on first. If it's cracked, broken, or even dirty, it sets the tone for the rest of the house.

Wash your driveway. (Use one of the many commercial cleaners available to get rid of stains.) If it's tar and it's badly cracked, have it resurfaced. This costs only a few hundred dollars. If the driveway is cement and it's cracked, have the cracked area cut out and replaced. Often you can replace a few sections of a cement driveway for a fraction of what it would cost for an entirely new driveway.

2. Manicure the Lawn and the Shrubs
Again, first impressions are critical. You want the lawn to look like a carpet, the shrubs not to have a branch out of place. Get lots of green showing; water heavily for a month or more before you put the place up for sale; plant flowers—you get the idea.

3. Paint the Front
No, it's not expensive to paint the front of your house. It's expensive to paint your whole house, but not to paint just the front. Most people

can do it themselves. Use high-quality paint and a complementary color on the trim.

Most important, repaint the front door. The first physical contact a potential buyer makes with your house is the front door.

4. Get Rid of Most of Your Furniture

Yes, you want to paint and clean inside, and we discussed that in Chapter 2. But the biggest inside mistake that most sellers make is to confuse a "lived in" look with a selling look.

Buyers like spaciousness. They want to be able to imagine how their furniture will look in your home. Never mind that once they move in, the house will be just as cluttered as it now is. You have to give them every opportunity to "see" themselves in your house.

Think of models for new homes that you may have seen. Did you notice that in the most charming models, the furniture was sparse— barely enough to live in, probably less than you'd find in the average hotel room?

You want to create an atmosphere of "negative space," where the rooms in your house cry out to be filled with more furniture— the buyer's furniture!

It doesn't matter what you do with most of your own furniture— put it in storage, leave it at a relative's or friend's house, store it, or burn it! Just get rid of it to help sell your home.

Technique 4: Offer Terms

What we all want is a buyer who comes in and gives us our price, in *cash*.

The trouble is that these days, few buyers have cash. Indeed, according to government statistics, we're a nation of consumers, not of savers. Exclusive of retirement accounts, less than 30 percent of the population has any sizable amount of cash savings at all—and many don't have enough to cover the down payment and closing costs when it comes time to buy a home.

Therefore, you can significantly increase the number of potential buyers for your home by offering to help them with the financing.

TIP—USE THE WORDS "SELLER FINANCING"

Anytime a buyer sees "seller financing" advertised or in a listing, it's a come-on. Immediately the buyer is more inclined to look at the property and to find a way to make an offer.

What is seller financing? Usually it means that you trade cash for paper (see Chapter 14). Instead of getting all cash, you carry back a second mortgage, usually for 10 percent or more of the selling price.

Do you want to sell faster and for more money? Offer the buyer financing. It makes your house much more desirable than those of other sellers who can't or won't offer financing. And you'll increase the potential number of buyers who will be interested.

Technique 5: Be Ready to Move Quickly or Slowly

After you sell, you plan to move out anyway, don't you? So, if buyers come along who say that they'll take your place and close escrow in 3 weeks, provided that you can move out by then, do it! You can always store your furniture temporarily and move into an apartment. But the important thing is that your house will be sold.

On the other hand, some buyers want a long escrow. They may not want to take possession for 90 or 120 days or more. They're waiting for their own home to close or for money to arrive from an inheritance, or they don't want to change schools in midyear. The point is, they want you to wait.

Should you? If the market's not superheated, chances are it will take you a couple of months, anyhow, to find another buyer. If these buyers are qualified for financing and make a noncontingent offer (so that they won't back out), and if they put up a big deposit, go for it.

Of course, any delay tends to threaten the sale. But if you're worried, you can always insist that you be allowed to continue showing the property and to accept backup offers from other buyers.

TRAP—IT AIN'T SOLD UNTIL IT'S SOLD!

My father, who worked in real estate for more than 35 years, used to say that he never felt sure that a property was sold until he received the check in his hand—and even then he still wasn't completely sure! There are no guaranteed sales, but sometimes you just have to take a chance on deals that look promising.

The Keys to Quick Sales

If you're fortunate enough to be able to offer buyers all five key inducements, you should have your house sold almost before the sign gets put up! They bear repeating.

Five Troubleshooting Keys to a Quick Sale

1. Help the neighborhood.
2. Offer a better price.
3. Improve the appearance of your home.
4. Offer terms.
5. Be ready to stay or move.

If you can't offer all five, offer four, or three, or two. What's important is that you give the buyer *at least one good reason* to purchase your property rather than someone else's. We live in a highly competitive society, and nowhere is that competition tougher than in real estate. If you want to get your house sold, you need an edge. That edge comes from going out of your way to make your property salable.

Remember, there's a buyer for every house. The only real question is, how long will it take that person to find your property?

GLOSSARY

Understanding the Terminology

If you're just being introduced to real estate, you'll quickly realize that people in this field have a language all their own. There are *points* and *disclosures* and *contingencies* and dozens of other terms that can make you think that people are talking in a foreign language.

Since buying a home is one of the biggest financial decisions in life, it's a good idea to become familiar with the following terms, which are frequently used in real estate. All too often, a lack of understanding can have very real consequences, such as confusion and failure to act (or taking an inappropriate action) on an important issue.

Abstract of title: A written document produced by a title insurance company (in some states an attorney will prepare it), giving the history of who owned the property from the first owner forward. It also indicates any liens or encumbrances that may affect the title. A lender will not make a loan, nor can a sale normally be concluded, until the title to real estate is clear, as evidenced by the abstract.

Acceleration clause: A clause that "accelerates" the payments on a mortgage, meaning that the entire amount becomes immediately due and payable. Most mortgages contain this clause (which kicks in if, for example, you sell the property).

Adjustable-rate mortgage (ARM): A mortgage whose interest rate fluctuates according to an index and a margin that are agreed to in advance by the borrower and the lender.

Adjustment date: The day on which an adjustment to an adjustable-rate mortgage is made. It may occur monthly, every six months, once a year, or as otherwise agreed.

Agent: Any person who is licensed to sell real estate, whether a broker or a salesperson.

Alienation clause: A clause in a mortgage specifying that if the property is transferred to another person, the mortgage becomes immediately due and payable. See also *Acceleration clause.*

ALTA: American Land Title Association. An organization offering a more complete and extensive title insurance policy. It involves a physical inspection and often guarantees the property's boundaries. Most lenders insist on an ALTA policy, with themselves named as beneficiary.

Amortization: Paying back the mortgage, both principal and interest, in equal installments. In other words, if the mortgage is for 30 years, you pay 360 equal installments. (The last payment is often a few dollars more or less.) This is the opposite of a mortgage with a balloon payment, which is a payment that is considerably larger than the rest. See *Balloon payment.*

Annual percentage rate (APR): The rate paid for a loan, including interest, loan fees, and points. This rate is determined by a government formula.

Appraisal: A valuation of a property, usually by a qualified appraiser. This is required by most lenders. The amount of the appraisal is the amount on which the maximum loan will be based. For example, if the appraisal is $100,000 and the lender is willing to lend 80 percent of value, the maximum mortgage will be $80,000.

ASA: American Society of Appraisers. A professional organization of appraisers.

As is: A property that is sold without warranties from the sellers. The sellers are essentially saying that they won't make any repairs.

Assignment of mortgage: The lender's sale of a mortgage, usually without the borrower's permission. For example, if you obtain a mortgage from XYZ Savings and Loan, and XYZ then sells the mortgage to Bland Bank, you will get a letter saying that the mortgage was assigned and that you are to make your payments to the new entity. The document used between lenders for the transfer is the "assignment of mortgage."

Assumption: Taking over an existing mortgage. If a seller has an assumable mortgage on a property, you can take over that seller's obligation under the loan when you buy the property. Most fixed-rate mortgages today are not assumable. Most adjustable-rate mortgages are assumable, but the borrower must qualify. FHA and VA mortgages may be assumable if certain conditions are met. When you assume the mortgage, you may be personally liable if there is a foreclosure.

Automatic guarantee: The power, which is given to some lenders, to guarantee Veterans Administration (VA) loans without first checking with the Veterans Administration. These lenders can often make these loans more quickly.

Backup: An offer that comes in after an earlier offer is accepted. If both buyer and seller agree, the backup offer assumes a secondary position, to be acted upon only if the original deal does not go through.

Balloon payment: A single mortgage payment, usually the last, that is larger than all the others. In the case of second mortgages held by sellers, often only interest is paid until the due date, then the entire amount borrowed (the principal) is due. See *Second mortgage.*

Biweekly mortgage: A mortgage on which payments are made every other week instead of monthly. Since there are 52 weeks in the year, you end up making 26 payments, or the equivalent of 1 extra month's payment. The additional payments, which are applied to the principal, significantly reduce the amount of interest charged on the mortgage and often reduce the term of the loan.

Blanket mortgage: A mortgage that covers several properties, instead of there being a single mortgage on each property. It is used most frequently by developers and builders.

Broker: An independent licensed agent, one who can establish his or her own office. Salespeople must work for brokers, typically for a few years, to get enough experience to become licensed as brokers.

Buy-down mortgage: A mortgage with a lower-than-market interest rate, either for the entire term of the mortgage or for a set period at the beginning—say, 2 years. The buy-down is made possible by the builder or seller's paying an up-front fee to the lender.

Buyer's agent: A real estate agent whose loyalty is to the buyer and not to the seller. Such agents are becoming increasingly common today.

Call provision: A clause in a mortgage that allows the lender to call in the entire unpaid balance of the loan if certain events, such as sale of the property, have occurred. See also *Acceleration clause.*

Canvass: To work a neighborhood, going through it and knocking on every door. Agents canvass to find listings. Investors and home buyers canvass to find potential sellers who have not yet listed their property—and may agree to sell quickly for less.

Caps: Limits put on an adjustable-rate mortgage. The interest rate, the monthly payment, or both may be capped.

CC&Rs: Covenants, conditions, and restrictions. These limit the activities that you as an owner may engage in. For example, you may be required to seek approval from a homeowners' association before adding onto your house or changing its color. Or you may be restricted from adding a second or third story to your home.

Certificate of reasonable value (CRV): A document issued by the Veterans Administration establishing what the VA feels is the property's maximum value. In some cases, if a buyer pays more than this amount for the property, he or she will not get a VA loan.

Chain of title: The history of ownership of the property. The title to property forms a chain going back to the first owners; in the Southwest, for example, these may have been the recipients of original Spanish land grants.

Closing: The process through which the seller conveys title to the buyer, the buyer makes full payment, including financing, for the property. At the closing, all required documents are signed and delivered and funds are disbursed.

Commission: The fee charged for an agent's services. Usually, but not always, the seller pays it. There is no set fee; rather, the amount is fully negotiable.

Commitment: A promise by a lender to issue a mortgage to a borrower at a set amount, interest rate, and cost. Typically, commitments have a time limit—for example, they are good for 5 or 15 days. Some lenders charge for making a commitment if you don't subsequently take out the mortgage (since they have tied up the money for that amount of time). When the lender's offer is in writing, it is sometimes called a firm commitment.

Conforming loan: A mortgage that conforms to the underwriting requirements of Fannie Mae or Freddie Mac.

Construction loan: A mortgage made for the purpose of constructing a building. The loan is short-term, typically under 12 months, and the money is usually paid in installments directly to the builder as the work is completed. Most often, such a loan is interest only.

Contingency: A condition that limits a contract. For example, the most common contingency says that a buyer is not required to complete a purchase if he or she fails to get the necessary financing. See also *Subject to.*

Conventional loan: Any loan that is not guaranteed or insured by the government.

Convertible mortgage: An adjustable-rate mortgage (ARM) with a clause allowing it to be converted to a fixed-rate mortgage at some time in the future. There may be an additional cost for obtaining this type of mortgage.

Cosigner: Someone with better credit (usually a close relative) who agrees to sign your loan if you do not have good enough credit to qualify for a mortgage. The cosigner is equally responsible for repayment of the loan. (If you don't pay it, the cosigner can be held liable for the entire balance.)

Credit report: A report, usually from one of the country's three large credit-reporting companies, that gives your credit history. It typically lists all your delinquent payments or failures to pay as well as any bankruptcies and, sometimes, foreclosures. Lenders use the report to determine whether to offer you a mortgage. The fee for obtaining the report is usually under $50, and you are charged for it.

Deal point: A point on which the deal hinges. It can be as important as the price or as trivial as changing the color of the mailbox.

Deposit: The money that buyers put up (also called *earnest money*) to demonstrate their seriousness in making an offer. The deposit is usually at risk if the buyers fail to complete the transaction and have no acceptable way of backing out of the deal.

Disclosures: A list and explanation of features of and defects in a property that sellers give to buyers. Most states now require disclosures.

Discount: The amount that a lender withholds from a mortgage to cover the points and fees. For example, if you borrow $100,000, but your points and fees come to $3000, the lender will fund only $97,000, discounting the $3000. Also, in the secondary market, the amount less than face value that a buyer of a mortgage pays as an inducement to take out the loan. The amount of the discount in this situation is determined by risk, market rates, the interest rate of the note, and other factors. See *Points*.

Dual agent: An agent who expresses loyalty to both buyers and sellers and agrees to work with both. Only a few agents can successfully play this role.

Due-on-encumbrance clause: A little-noticed and seldom-enforced clause in recent mortgages that allows the lender to foreclose if the borrower gets additional financing. For example, if you secure a second mortgage, the lender of the first mortgage may have grounds for foreclosing. The reasoning here is that if you reduce your equity level by taking out additional financing, the lender may be placed in a less secure position.

Due-on-sale clause: A clause in a mortgage specifying that the entire unpaid balance becomes due and payable upon the sale of the property. See *Acceleration clause*.

Escrow company: An independent third party (stakeholder) that handles funds; carries out the instructions of the lender, buyer, and seller in a transaction; and deals with all the documents. In most states, companies are licensed to handle escrows. In some parts of the country, particularly the Northeast, the functions of the escrow company may be handled by an attorney.

FHA loan: A mortgage insured by the Federal Housing Administration. In most cases, the FHA advances no money, but instead insures a loan made by a lender such as a bank. There is a fee to the borrower for this insurance, which is usually paid up front.

Fixed-rate mortgage: A mortgage whose interest rate does not fluctuate over the life of the loan.

Fixer-upper: A home that does not show well and is in bad shape. Often the property is euphemistically referred to in listings as a "TLC" (needs tender loving care) or "handyman's special."

Foreclosure: A legal proceeding in which the lender takes possession and title to a property, usually after the borrower fails to make timely payments on a mortgage.

Fannie Mae: The Federal National Mortgage Association, a secondary lender.

Freddie Mac: The Federal Home Loan Mortgage Corporation, a secondary lender.

FSBO: For sale by owner.

Garbage fees: Extra (and often unnecessary) charges tacked on when a buyer obtains a mortgage.

Graduated-payment mortgage: A mortgage whose payments vary over the life of the loan. They start out low, then slowly rise until, usually after a few years, they reach a plateau, where they remain for the balance of the term. Such a mortgage is particularly useful when you want low initial payments. It is primarily used by first-time buyers, often in combination with a fixed-rate or adjustable-rate mortgage.

Growing equity mortgage: A rarely used type of mortgage whose payments increase according to a set schedule. The purpose is to pay additional money toward principal and thus pay off the loan earlier and save interest charges.

HOA: Homeowners' association, found mainly in condos but also in some single-family areas. It represents homeowners and establishes and maintains neighborhood architectural and other standards. You usually must get permission from the HOA to make significant external changes to your property.

Index: A measurement of an established interest rate used to determine the periodic adjustments for adjustable-rate mortgages. There are a wide variety of indexes, including Treasury bill rates and the cost of funds to lenders.

Inspection: A physical survey of the property to determine if there are any problems or defects.

Jumbo: A mortgage for more than the maximum amount of a conforming loan.

Lien: A claim against real estate for money owed by the owner. For example, if you had work done on your property and refused to pay the worker, he or she might file a "mechanic's lien" against your property. If you didn't pay taxes, the taxing agency might file a "tax lien." These liens cloud the title and usually prevent you from selling or refinancing the property until they are cleared by paying off the debt.

Loan-to-value ratio (LTV): The percentage of the appraised value of a property that a lender will loan. For example, if your property is appraised at

$100,000 and the lender is willing to loan $80,000, the loan-to-value ratio is 80 percent.

Lock in: To establish the interest rate for a mortgage in advance of actually getting it. For example, a buyer might "lock in" a mortgage at 7.5 percent, so that if rates subsequently were to rise, he or she would still get that rate. Sometimes there's a fee for this. It's always a good idea to get it in writing from the lender, just to be sure that if rates rise, the lender doesn't change its mind.

Lowball: To make a very low initial offer to purchase.

MAI: Member, American Institute of Real Estate Appraisers. An appraiser with this designation has completed rigorous training.

Margin: An amount, calculated in points, that a lender adds to an index to determine how much interest you will pay during a period for an adjustable-rate mortgage. For example, if index is at 7 percent and the margin, which was agreed upon at the time you obtained the mortgage, is 2.7 points, the interest rate for that period is 9.7 percent. See also *Index, Points*.

Median sales price: The midpoint of the price of homes—as many properties have sold above this price as have sold below it.

MLS: Multiple Listing Service—used by Realtors as a listings exchange. Nearly 90 percent of all homes listed in the country are found on the MLS.

Mortgage: A loan arrangement between a borrower, or *mortgagor*, and a lender, or *mortgagee*. If you don't make your payments on a mortgage, the lender can foreclose, or take ownership of the property, only by going to court. This court action can take a great deal of time, often 6 months or more. Furthermore, even after the lender has taken back the property, you may have an "equity of redemption" for years afterward that allows you to redeem the property by paying back the mortgage and the lender's costs.

The length of time that it takes to foreclose, the costs involved, and the equity of redemption make a mortgage much less desirable to lenders than a trust deed.

Mortgage banker: A lender that specializes in offering mortgages but none of the other services normally provided by a bank.

Mortgage broker: A company that specializes in providing "retail" mortgages to consumers. It usually represents many different lenders.

Motivated seller: A seller who has a strong desire to sell. For example, the seller may have been transferred and must move quickly.

Multiple counteroffers: Comeback offers extended by the seller to several buyers simultaneously.

Multiple offers: Offers for the same property that are submitted simultaneously by several buyers.

Negative amortization: A condition that arises when the payment on an adjustable-rate mortgage is not sufficiently large to cover the interest charged. The excess interest is then added to the principal, so that the amount borrowed actually increases. The amount by which the principal can increase is usually limited to 125 percent of the original mortgage value. Any mortgage that includes payment caps has the potential for negative amortization.

Origination fee: An expense for obtaining a mortgage. Originally, it was a charge that lenders made for preparing and submitting a mortgage. The fee applied only to FHA and VA loans, which had to be submitted to the government for approval. With an FHA loan, the maximum origination fee was 1 percent.

Personal property: Any property that does not go with the land. Such property includes automobiles, clothing, and most furniture. Some items, such as appliances and floor and wall coverings, are disputable. See also *Real property*.

PITI: Principal, interest, taxes, and insurance. These are the major components that go into determining the monthly payment on a mortgage. (Other items include homeowners' association dues and utilities.)

Points: 1 percent of a mortgage amount, payable on obtaining the loan. For example, if your mortgage is $100,000 and you are required to pay 2½ points to get it, the charge to you is $2500. Some points may be tax deductible. Check with your accountant.

A "basis point" is $\frac{1}{100}$ of a point. For example, if you are charged ½ point (0.5 percent of the mortgage), the lender may refer to it as 50 basis points.

Preapproval: Formal approval for a mortgage from a lender. You have to submit a standard application and have a credit check. Also, the lender may require proof of income, employment, and money on deposit (to be used for the down payment and closing costs).

Prepayment penalty: A charge demanded by the lender from the borrower for paying off a mortgage early. In times past (more than 25 years ago), nearly all mortgages carried prepayment penalties. However, those mortgages were also assumable by others. Today virtually no fixed-rate mortgages (other than FHA and VA mortgages) are truly assumable; however, some do carry a prepayment penalty clause. See *Assumption*.

Private mortgage insurance (PMI): Insurance that protects the lender in the event that the borrower defaults on a mortgage. It is written by an independent third-party insurance company and typically covers only the first 20 percent of the lender's potential loss. PMI is normally required on any mortgage with a loan-to-value ratio greater than 80 percent.

Purchase money mortgage: A mortgage obtained as part of the purchase price of a home (usually from the seller), as opposed to a mortgage obtained through refinancing.

In some states, no deficiency judgment can be obtained against the borrower of a purchase money mortgage. (That is, if there is a foreclosure and the property brings less than the amount borrowed, the borrower cannot be held liable for the shortfall.)

Real property: Real estate. This includes the land and anything appurtenant to it, including the house. Certain tests have been devised to determine whether an item is real property (i.e., whether it goes with the land). For example, if curtains or drapes have been attached in such a way that they cannot be removed without damaging the home, they may be spoken of as real property. On the other hand, if they can easily be removed without damaging the home, they may be personal property. The purchase agreement should specify whether doubtful items are real or personal property to avoid confusion later on.

Realtor: A broker who is a member of the National Association of Realtors. Agents who are not members may not use the Realtor designation.

REO: Real estate owned—a term that refers to property taken back through foreclosure and held for sale by a lender.

RESPA: Real Estate Settlement Procedures Act. Legislation requiring lenders to provide borrowers with specified information on the cost of securing financing. Basically, it means that before you proceed far along the path of getting the mortgage, the lender has to provide you with an estimate of costs. Then, before you sign the documents binding you to the mortgage, the lender has to provide you with a breakdown of the actual costs.

Second mortgage: An inferior mortgage, usually placed on the property after a first mortgage. In the event of foreclosure, the second mortgage is paid off only after the first mortgage has been fully paid. Many lenders will not offer second mortgages.

Short sale: A property sale in which a lender agrees to accept less than the mortgage amount in order to facilitate the sale and avoid a foreclosure.

SREA: Society of Real Estate Appraisers—a professional association to which qualified appraisers can belong.

Subject to: A phrase often used to indicate that a buyer is not assuming the mortgage liability of a seller. For example, if the seller has an assumable loan and you (the buyer) assume the loan, you are taking over liability for payment. On the other hand, if you purchase "subject to" the mortgage, you do not assume liability for payment.

Subordination clause: A clause in a mortgage document that keeps the mortgage subordinate to another mortgage.

Title: Legal evidence that you actually have the right of ownership of real property. It is given in the form of a deed (there are many different types of deeds) that specifies the kind of title you have (joint, common, or other).

Title insurance policy: An insurance policy that covers the title to a home. It may list the owner or the lender as beneficiary. The policy is issued by a title insurance company and specifies that if for any covered reason your title proves to be defective, the company will correct the title or compensate you up to a specified amount, usually the amount of the purchase price or the mortgage.

Trust deed: A three-party lending arrangement that includes a borrower, or "trustor"; an independent third-party stakeholder, or "trustee" (usually a title insurance company); and a lender, or "beneficiary," so called because the lender stands to benefit if the trustee turns over the deed in the event that the borrower fails to make payments. The advantage of the trust deed over the mortgage is that foreclosure can be accomplished without court action or a deficiency judgment against the borrower. (In other words, if the property is worth less than the loan, the lender can't come back to the borrower after the sale for the difference.) See also *Purchase money mortgage.*

Upgrade: Any extra that a buyer may obtain when purchasing a new home—for example, a better-quality carpet or a wall mirror in the bedroom.

Upside down: Owing more on a property than its market value.

VA loan: A mortgage guaranteed by the Veterans Administration. The VA actually guarantees only a small percentage of the loan amount, but since it guarantees the "top" of the monies loaned, lenders are willing to accept the arrangement. In a VA loan, the government advances no money; rather, the mortgage is made by a private lender, such as a bank.

Wraparound financing: A blend of two mortgages, often used by sellers to get a higher interest rate or facilitate a sale. For example, instead of giving a buyer a simple second mortgage, the seller may combine the balance due on an existing mortgage (usually an existing first) with an additional loan. Thus the wrap includes both the second and the first mortgages. The borrower makes payments to the seller, who then keeps part of the payment and pays off the existing mortgage.

RESOURCES

Robert Irwin, www.robertirwin.com. The author's web site.

Government Agencies

Housing and Urban Development, www.hud.gov. Information on government programs, including those involving settlement and closing procedures.

Federal Housing Administration, http://www.hud.gov/offices/hsg/index.cfm. Information on FHA loan insurance and housing programs.

Veterans Administration, www.va.gov. Information on VA loan guarantees and housing programs.

Secondary Lenders

Fannie Mae, www.fanniemae.com and www.homepath.com. Information on loans, settlement procedures, and foreclosures.

Freddie Mac, www.freddiemac.com. Information on loans and settlement procedures.

Ginnie Mae, www.ginniemae.gov. Information on home purchasing and ownership.

Credit Bureaus and Organizations

Consumer Data Industry Associations, http://www.cdiaonline.org/. Information on credit reports and credit laws.

Equifax, www.equifax.com. National credit reporting agency.

Experian, www.experian.com. National credit reporting agency.

Fair Isaac (credit scores), www.fairisaac.com. The main credit scoring organization.

Federal Trade Commission, www.ftc.gov. The agency that handles credit-reporting complaints.

Trans Union, www.transunion.com. National credit reporting agency.

Title Insurance/Escrow Organizations

American Escrow Association, http://www.a-e-a.org. A major escrow trade association.

American Land Title Associations, www.alta.org. A major title association and trade association.

California Escrow Association, www.ceaescrow.org. California's trade escrow association.

California Land Title Association, www.clta.org/store/forms/homeown.pdf. California's title association.

Chicago Title Insurance Company, www.ctic.com. A major title insurance company.

First American Title Insurance Company, http://firstam.com. A major title insurance company.

Illinois Land Title Association, www.illinoislandtitle.org. The Illinois title insurance association.

Texas Land Title Association, www.tlta.com. The Texas title insurance association.

Home Inspection Organizations

American Institute of Inspectors, www.inspection.org. A home inspection trade association.

American Society of Home Inspectors, www.ashi.com. A large national home inspection trade association. It encourages high standards for inspectors. Most important, it offers a written list of inspection criteria by which an inspector should judge your property. This list is quite extensive and helps provide for a more thorough inspection.

National Association of Certified Home Inspectors, www.nachi.org. Another national home inspector trade association that also encourages high standards for its members. Ask if your inspector is a member.

Other Related Organizations

Dataquick, www.dataquick.com. Provides information on real estate (fees).

National Association of Realtors, www.realtor.com or www.realtor.org. Provides information on members, homes for sale, and other data.

The Legal Description, www.thelegaldescription.com. Provides information on legal news regarding home closings.

Index

211

214   Index

About the Author

Robert Irwin, noted real estate broker for more than three decades, and the author of the best-selling Tips & Traps real estate series, serves as a consultant to lenders, investors, and brokers. With over 50 books, including *How to Get Started in Real Estate Investing* and *How to Find Hidden Real Estate Bargains,* Irwin is recognized as one of the most knowledgeable writers in the real estate field.